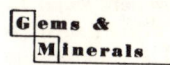

GEM CUTTER'S HANDBOOK

SPECIAL GEMSTONE SHAPES

The beginning gem cutter will find that an oval is the easiest shape to cut. Later he will want to try rectangles, crosses, hearts, etc. Two of the most difficult shapes are rectangles and circles. If a drill press is available, abrasive core drills can be used to cut out circular preforms (see preforming gems). There are tricks to cutting other shapes that can make them easier.

This section covers shaping and finishing. The sections on preforming and trim sawing should be consulted for preliminary steps. For several of the shapes it is necessary that grinding wheels be true, with squared edges. The section on grinding shows how to dress wheels that do not meet these requirements.

The Loaf

The loaf is a rectangle with flat ends and a modified cylindrical top. Like all rectangular stones, much time and effort is saved if the preform is sawed with straight parallel edges intersecting at 90 degrees. The lower portion of the stone is ground in a straight bezel bevel with an angle of about 15 degrees. The normal height of the bezel bevel is 1/3 that of the stone, but this varies according to the bezel height of different mountings.

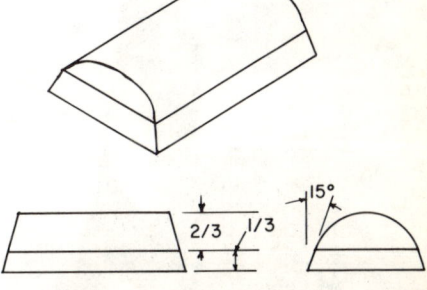

Grinding wheels must be flat faced, true, and free of grooves to cut rectangular stones. To make sure the gem's edges stay straight, move the stone diagonally across the surface of the wheel. To avoid grooving the wheel, be sure to use its entire surface.

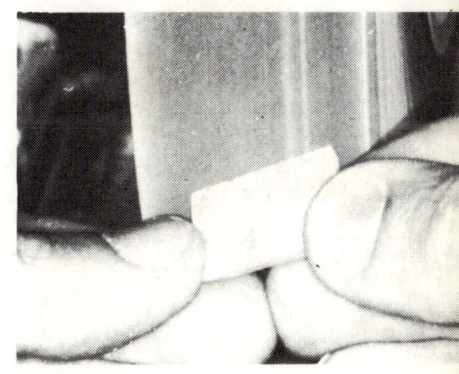

1 — ADVANCED CABOCHON CUTTING

A good way to make sure that edges are ground straight and perpendicular to each other is to use a device such as Brad's Polygon Master. The square plate at the base of the dop makes it possible to cut any rectangular shape. A home-made device for the same purpose can be made from Tinker Toys (see the grinding section).

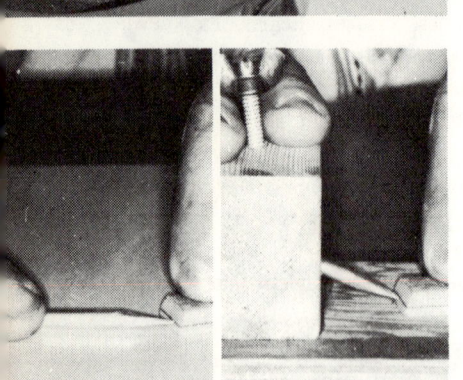

When the bevelled sides have been ground, the height of the bezel bevel should be marked with an aluminum or brass wire pencil. Since this height will vary from mounting to mounting, an adjustable holder for the pencil is very handy. To make the holder, a small block of wood is nailed to a piece of $1/4$ inch plywood. An angling hole for the pencil is drilled. By moving the pencil in and out, the height of the mark can be varied. A vertical hole for a set screw can be drilled and tapped into the block.

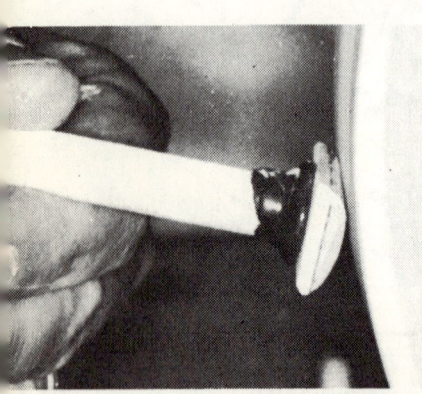

After marking, dop the stone and grind off the top so that the curve extends from one long side to the other. The curve should start above the bezel bevel at about 20 degrees. Grinding the crown so that it has a perfect curve and is parallel to the sides requires some skill. Keep your hands steady and sweep the stone in an arc across the surface of the grinding wheel. In sanding, take care to keep the edges straight and the crown properly curved and parallel. Polish as you would any cabochon.

Cutting a Cross

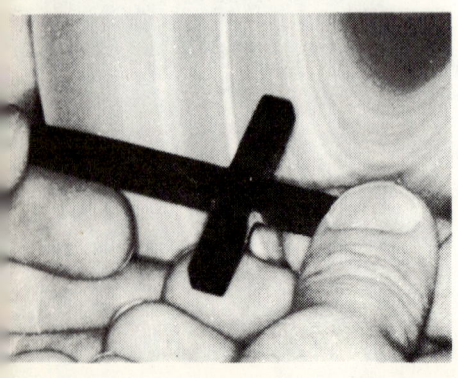

A stone cross is a popular form with gem cutters. Refer to the trim sawing section for methods of cutting out the preform. To grind this shape, it is mandatory that the sides and face of the grinding wheel be true and at right angles. Grind the edges on a coarse wheel, checking frequently to make sure the bars are at 90 degrees to each other. Do not grind a curve into the edge. Finish grinding on a fine grit wheel.

ADVANCED CABOCHON CUTTING — 2

The edges of the cross are most easily sanded on rubber bonded abrasive wheels. Like grinding wheels, the rubber ones should be trued. Use at least two grits, coarse and fine. An extra fine wheel may be used for final smoothing. Run the wheels wet.

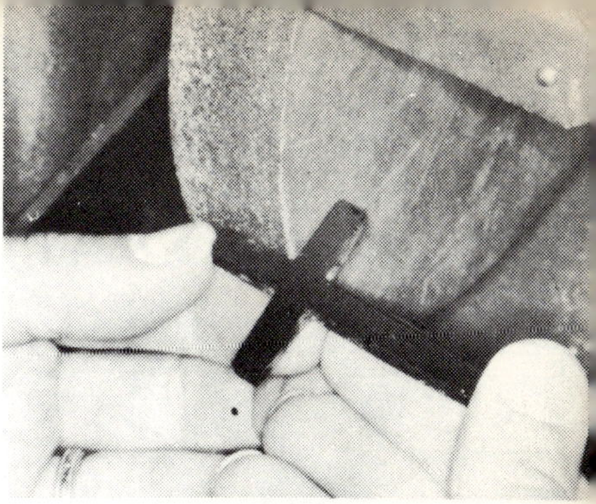

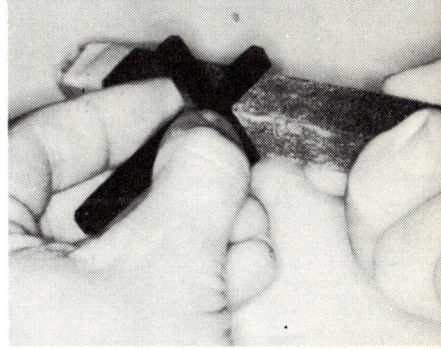

A drum sander may also be used for smoothing the edges. However, the edges of the sanding cloth usually curl under pressure so that the inside corners of the cross are not finished. To finish the corners, fasten some abrasive cloth around a square stick and sand by hand. After smoothing, polish the edges. A hard felt wheel will get into the corners.

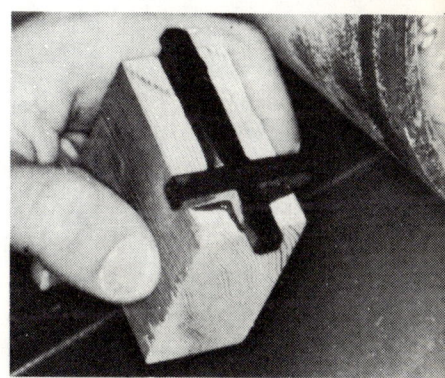

To smooth and polish the front, dop the stone on a block just slightly smaller than the cross. Either rubber bonded wheels or a drum sander can be used for smoothing. Bevel the corners slightly to avoid chipping. Polish the front when it is properly smoothed. Then remove the cross from the block and re-dop for finishing the back. If the cross is to be worn, make it of some tough material such as jade. Crosses are usually drilled at the top for ring mountings (drilling is covered in *Specialized Gem Cutting*).

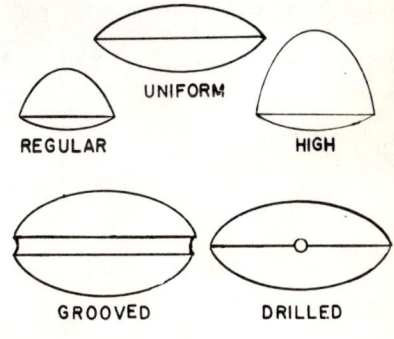

Double Cabochons

Most cabochons cut by amateurs have flat backs. A double cabochon has a domed surface on each side of the plane formed by the girdle. Transparent and semitransparent stones are especially attractive cut as double cabochons with the top of the stone a regular high dome and the back a shallow dome. This lenticular form concentrates the light and reflects it back to improve the color and brilliance of the stone. The girdle may be left sharp for regular and cinch mountings, grooved for suspension, or drilled for a loop mounting.

REGULAR   UNIFORM   HIGH

GROOVED   DRILLED

3 — ADVANCED CABOCHON CUTTING

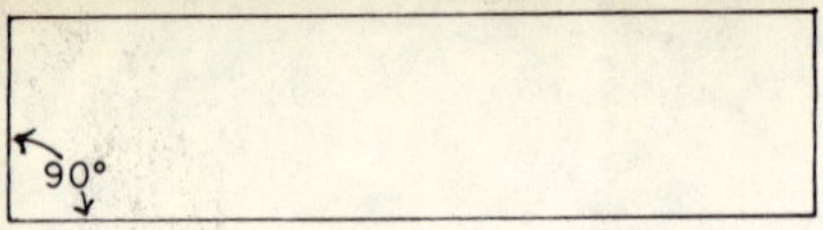

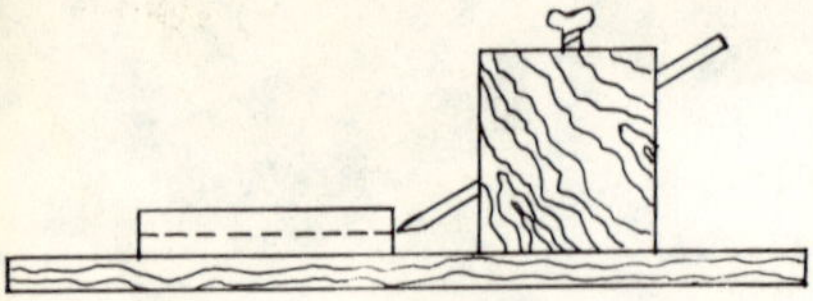

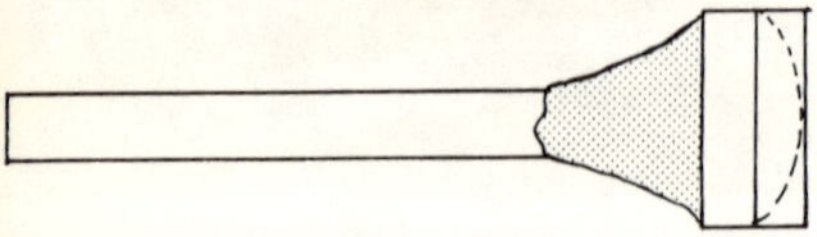

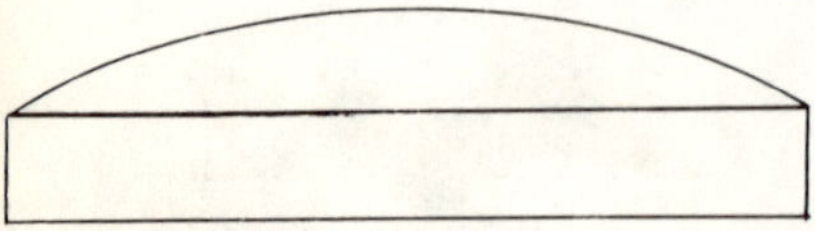

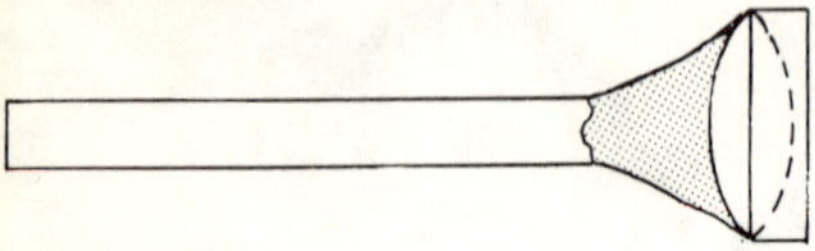

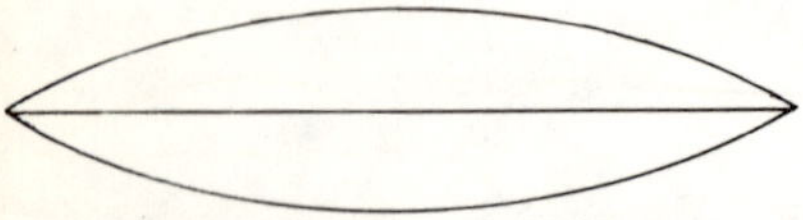

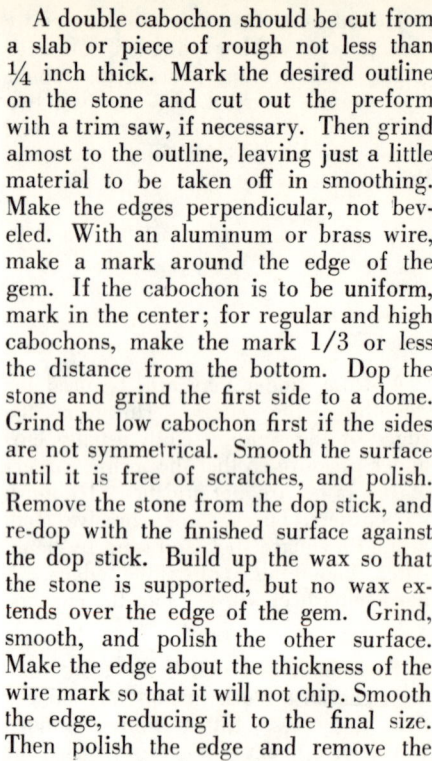

A double cabochon should be cut from a slab or piece of rough not less than 1/4 inch thick. Mark the desired outline on the stone and cut out the preform with a trim saw, if necessary. Then grind almost to the outline, leaving just a little material to be taken off in smoothing. Make the edges perpendicular, not beveled. With an aluminum or brass wire, make a mark around the edge of the gem. If the cabochon is to be uniform, mark in the center; for regular and high cabochons, make the mark 1/3 or less the distance from the bottom. Dop the stone and grind the first side to a dome. Grind the low cabochon first if the sides are not symmetrical. Smooth the surface until it is free of scratches, and polish. Remove the stone from the dop stick, and re-dop with the finished surface against the dop stick. Build up the wax so that the stone is supported, but no wax extends over the edge of the gem. Grind, smooth, and polish the other surface. Make the edge about the thickness of the wire mark so that it will not chip. Smooth the edge, reducing it to the final size. Then polish the edge and remove the stone from the dop stick.

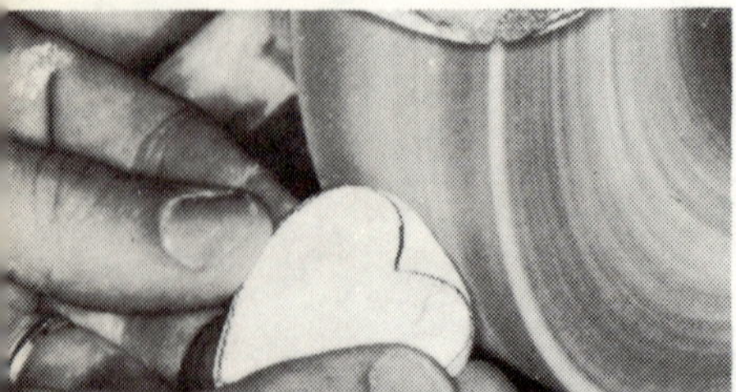

Hearts

Gemstone hearts are sometimes cut with flat backs for setting in heart shaped mountings, but more often as double cabochons. Mark the shape and trim out the preform. Grind around the stone leaving just a little material outside the mark for finishing. For a double cabochon, hold the stone so that the edges are cut at 90 degrees. Cut the usual 10 or 15 degree bevel for a flat backed cabochon. Do not grind into the notch at the top until the next step.

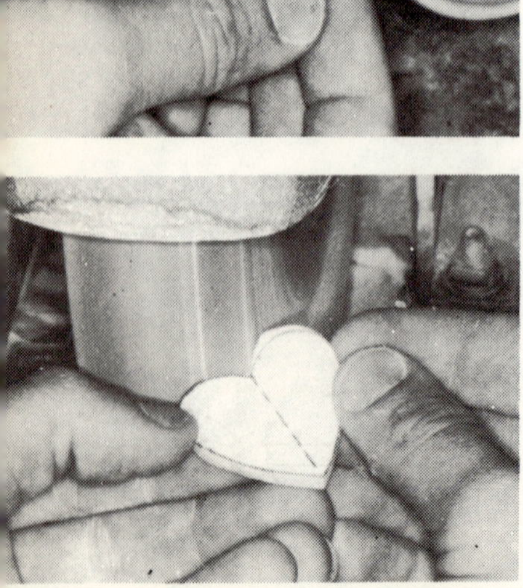

To cut the notch, push the stone against the sharp corner of the wheel. The stone should be held so that an imaginary line from the point of the heart to the center of the notch is at 45 degrees to the face of the wheel. Round off the shoulder at the top.

ADVANCED CABOCHON CUTTING — 4

To cut the heart as a double cabochon, make a mark in the center of the edge around the periphery of the stone. To make sure the mark is in the center, turn the stone over after marking once and mark again. This will give a good clear thick mark. When the stone is ground, leave the thickness of the mark for a girdle that will not chip. Dop the stone for grinding the first surface.

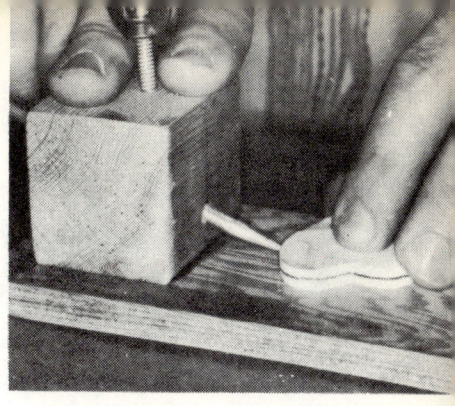

Grind from the edge toward the center of the stone. The arrows in the drawing show the directions from which the stone is ground. Note that no attempt is made to grind outward from the center of the notch. Grinding in this direction produces a groove in the face of the stone which cannot be removed. After the first face is profiled, smooth and polish. Remove the heart from the dop stick, redop and repeat the process. For flat backed hearts, the second step is eliminated. The drawings show the profiles of double and flat backed hearts.

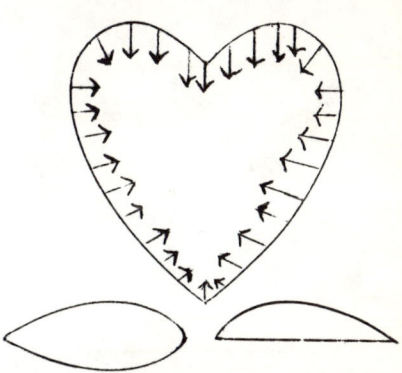

The edges are easily sanded on rubber bonded abrasive wheels. The edge of a drum sander may also be used, but it may be necessary to finish the center of the notch by hand. A hard felt wheel works best for polishing the edge, but other types of buffs may be used. Take care in smoothing and polishing that you do not snag the point of the heart on the wheel. Double cabochon hearts may be drilled for a peg bail or ring, or a cement-on bail may be used to make an attractive pendant.

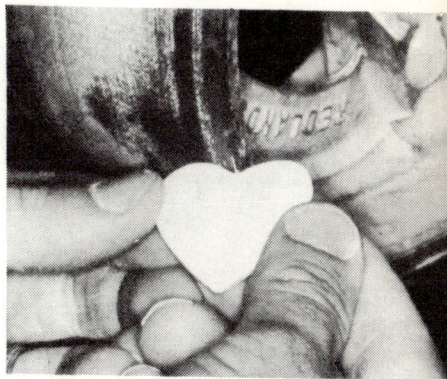

Teardrops

Teardrops are handled much the same as hearts, and are usually cut as double cabochons. They may be drilled through the top for bails or rings, or set in one of the commercial teardrop mountings. Another method of mounting is to grind a flat spot on the tip and drill for an eye. Cement-on ring mountings known as *up eyes* may also be attached to the flattened tip. In grinding and smoothing a teardrop, the small end cuts faster and sometimes drags on the wheel. Use lighter pressure.

5 — ADVANCED CABOCHON CUTTING

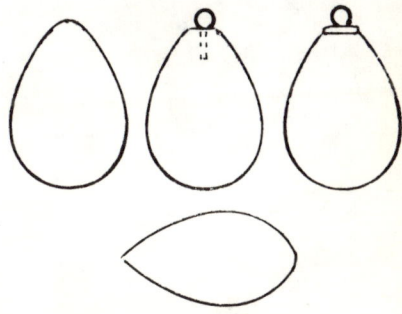

PROFILE

Star Shaped Stones

For a star, first cut a circular preform. If you have an abrasive tube drill (see preforming section) you can save yourself some time and effort. Otherwise, trim out a preform and cut the circle with a grinding wheel. Make the edges of the stone perpendicular to the faces.

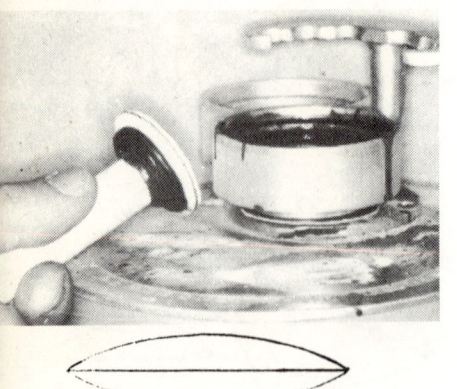

Make a center mark around the edge of the stone. Then dop and grind the profile, almost to the center mark. Remove the stone from the dop stick and re-dop to profile the other face. The result is a round, uniform double cabochon.

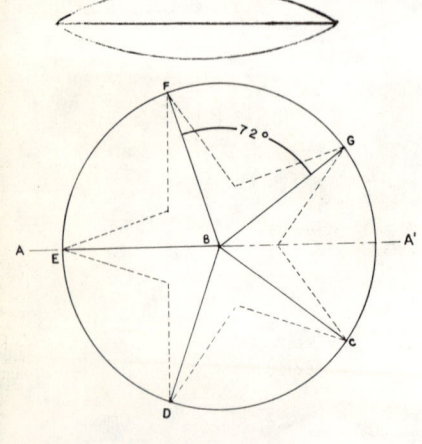

Making the Star Template

From a point on a line drawn on paper, measure off angles of 72 degrees. Draw five radiating lines at these angles. Place the point of a compass at the central point on the line and scribe a circle just slightly smaller than the double cabochon stone disc. Cut out the paper circle.

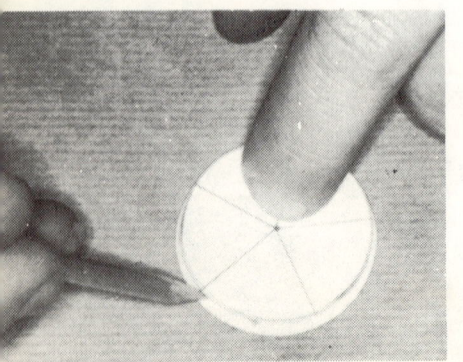

Place the circular template on the gem and mark off the five points on the stone disc.

ADVANCED CABOCHON CUTTING — 6

Lay a flexible steel rule on the stone and draw lines from each point to an opposite point. This will give you a perfect star pattern. The flexible rule is used because it conforms to the domed shape of the stone.

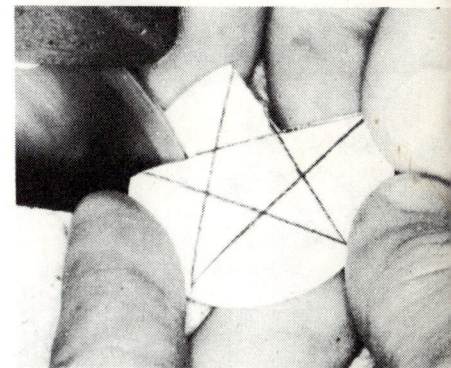

Cut out the points on a trim saw. To make sure you do not cut too far into the under side of the gem, tilt up the back. A wedge like that shown in the trim sawing section for cutting crosses can be used to advantage; it's safer than holding the stone by hand. Saw a little outside the star's outline.

Grind the point edges to the outline on a 220 grit wheel. Hold the stone at 90 degrees to the face of the wheel. Check frequently to make sure that you are cutting accurately. The wheel must be true and have sharp corners. *Note: Instead of trim sawing the points, it is possible to cut them entirely on a grinding wheel. Start with coarse grit and finish with fine. It's a slower process, but safe.*

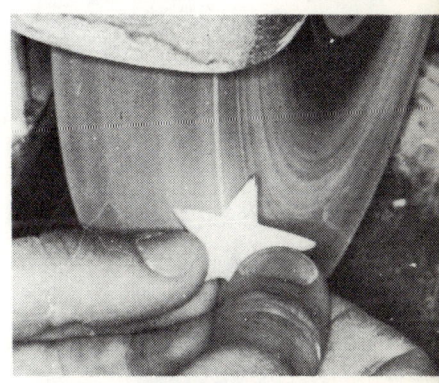

Smooth the edges with rubber bonded wheels or a drum sander. If a drum sander is used, inside corners may have to be hand sanded as in cutting crosses. Carefully blunt the star's points slightly so that they will not chip. Polish the edges, preferably on a hard felt wheel.

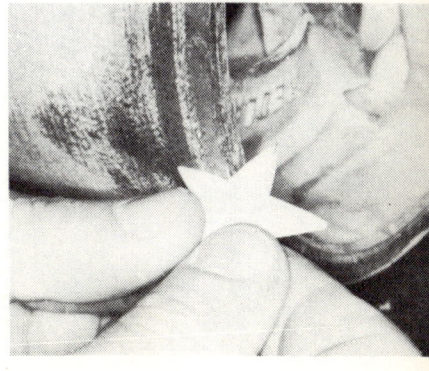

7 — ADVANCED CABOCHON CUTTING

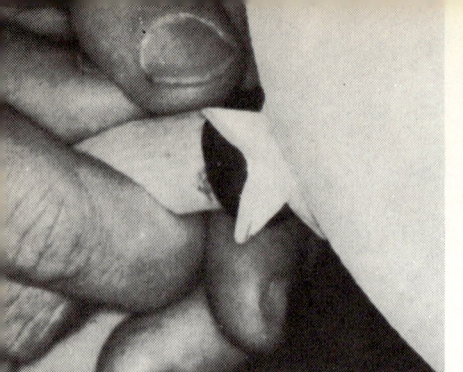

Dop the star on a large dop stick and smooth the exposed surface. Then polish. Take care that the points do not snag the sanding cloth or buff. Always smooth and polish toward the trailing edge of the stone.

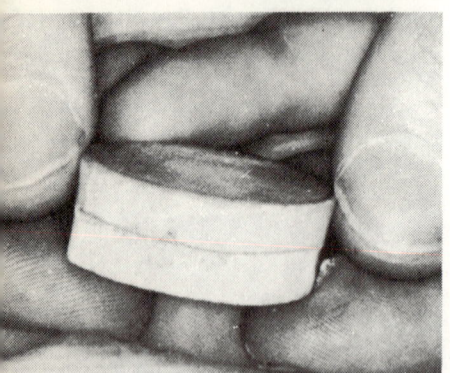

Some Cabochon Tricks

Cutting two stones of identical shape and size can be made easier by cementing two preforms together with a Peel 'Em Off type of cement. Then grind to the outline with the edges perpendicular to the faces. Soak in hot water to loosen the stones, remove the cement with cleaning fluid and dop the gems. Then bevel the edges, and cut the tops to the cabochon shape.

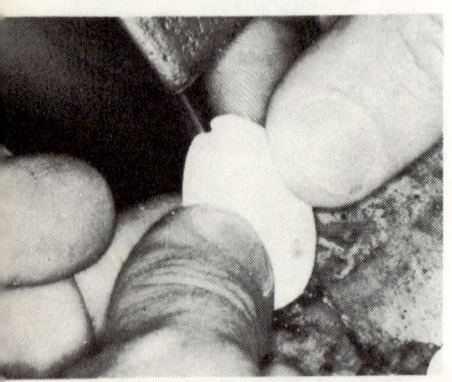

Beads may be made on standard equipment by first cutting two identical cabochons. Do not chamfer the bottom edges; leave them sharp. With the edge of a diamond saw, cut a groove about 1/32 inch deep across the base of each stone along the center line.

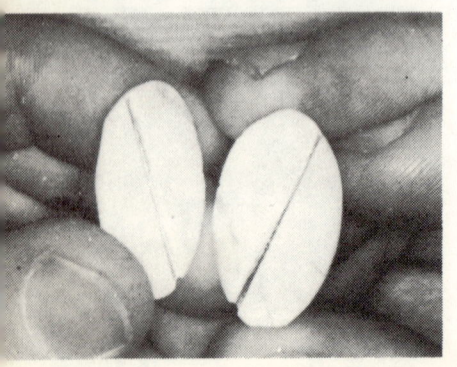

Cement the cabochons together with epoxy, being careful to match the grooves. When the cement has hardened, smooth the edges to even up, and polish. If there is epoxy in the hole, drill it out with a regular drill bit.

ADVANCED CABOCHON CUTTING — 8

Gems & Minerals

GEM CUTTER'S HANDBOOK
ASSEMBLED STONES
Cabochon Backings, Doublets, Triplets

To strengthen a gemstone, or enhance its beauty, it is sometimes desirable to cement the gem to another material. Various backings are occasionally used to add color to clear stones. Pale asteriated rose quartz is frequently backed with colored mirrors to enhance the star or to simulate star sapphires.

The most common assembled stone is the opal doublet. Beautiful opal is often found in seams too thin to cut into cabochons. The thin opal is cemented to a backing material. A cabochon is then cut from this assembly. Another type of doublet is made by cementing a thin piece of opal or other colorful material to a protective cap of clear quartz. This technique is used to protect soft or easily damaged material.

Triplets are assembled from three pieces of material. A popular triplet is made from a clear quartz cap, a thin layer of opal, and a thin backing layer of black obsidian.

Doublets and triplets are not imitations or fakes. A piece of asteriated quartz backed by a blue mirror is a fake if it is labeled as a star sapphire. However, an opal doublet is a genuine stone backed by a strengthening material. Many attractive, thin stones could never be cut and enjoyed if it were not for this process.

Cementing Assembled Stones

Various adhesives such as Canada balsam, stick shellac, jeweler's thermosetting cement, and dop wax have been used for cementing assembled stones. Today, epoxy cement is commonly used. In cementing clear stones, be careful that no air bubbles are trapped in the cement. They will show through as silver spots. To eliminate air, try coating one surface with epoxy resin, and the other with an equal amount of catalyst. Then press the two pieces of material together. It's a good idea to clamp them until the cement has set. In clamping, be careful not to apply too much pressure on thin pieces.

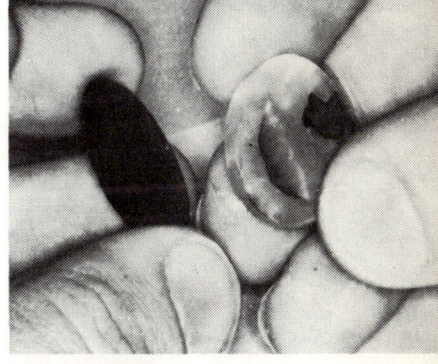

Backings

Novelty gems may be made by backing transparent stones with a reflective material. One hobbyist likes to back clear cabochons with Scotchlite reflective sheeting. (Scotchlite is available from sign and auto supply houses in a variety of colors). Anodized aluminum may also be used for a colored backing. Set these gems in bezel mountings with solid backs.

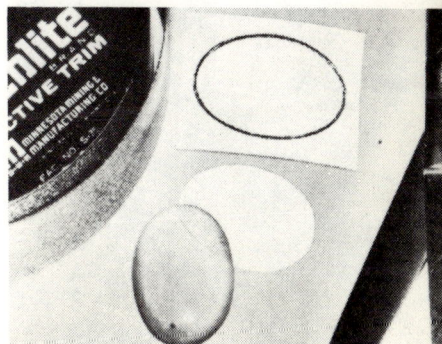

9 — ADVANCED CABOCHON CUTTING

Transparent jelly opals with play of fire often require an opaque backing to bring out the flashes of color. Some cutters coat the backs of these gems with epoxy cement to which black coloring pigment has been added. Black lacquer may also be used.

Colored mirrors are sometimes used to back clear stones, especially star quartz. (Cutting star stones will be covered in a subsequent section). With grinding and smoothing wheels, cut a piece of mirror to the size and shape of the cabochon. Then cement the mirror and stone together. Since colored mirrors are sometimes difficult to obtain, you can use a clear mirror and dyed epoxy. The transparent dye used for coloring plastic resin works well. For a novel effect, try one color of cement in the center and another color around the edge. (Note: cabochons to which backings are to be cemented should be lapped through 400 grit on the underside, but not polished. Polish only the top.)

Simulated cat's-eye and star stones can be made by backing clear cabochons with pieces of specially prepared aluminum. To prepare the aluminum, cut a piece to the size and shape of the cabochon. Then lay the aluminum on a flat surface, and abrade it lightly with a fine piece of emery cloth wrapped around a square stick. The finer the abrasive cloth, the better. The scratches must be perfectly straight; lay a straight edge on the flat surface next to the aluminum for a guide. If you want a cat's-eye effect, abrade in one direction only. Four-rayed stars are made by making two sets of scratches at 90 degrees to each other. For six-rayed stars, make three sets of scratches at 120 degrees to each other. Cement the backing to the clear cabochon with clear or dyed epoxy.

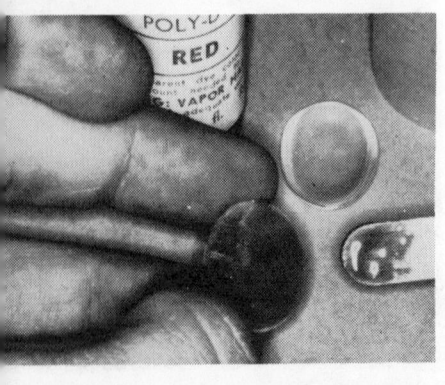

ADVANCED CABOCHON CUTTING — 10

Attractive jewelry items may be made by cementing small freeform shaped cabochons of opal or other colorful material to large cabochons of obsidian or jade. Cut the large cabochon with a fairly flat crown. Polish the large stone, and then rough up the spot where the small cabochon will be cemented with a piece of 220 or 400 grit abrasive cloth. The small cabochon should have a flat back that has been lapped with 400 grit. Cement the stones together with epoxy.

Opal Doublets

To make an opal doublet, select a thin piece of opal showing plenty of play of color. If there is any matrix on the surface, grind this away on the face of the grinding wheel. Check frequently to determine the direction of the bands of color. The bands often run diagonally from the top to the bottom of the stone. If the stone's thickness permits, grind a top and bottom surface parallel to the band and to each other. On the periphery of the wheel, make these surfaces as flat as possible. Check frequently to determine when the top surface is in the most attractive color band. Do not grind too far into the band so that material will be left for smoothing. Finish grinding the surfaces on the side of the grinding wheel, using plenty of water. Check the color bands frequently. Opal cuts rapidly; it's best to grind on a fine grit wheel. The flat surfaces can also be processed on a lap plate with fine grit and a light, careful touch.

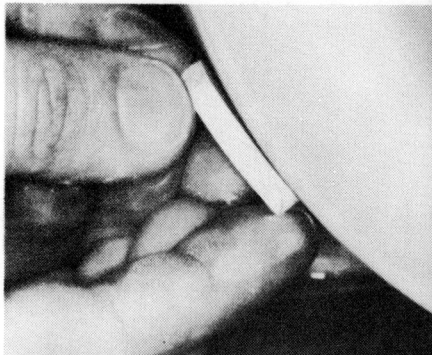

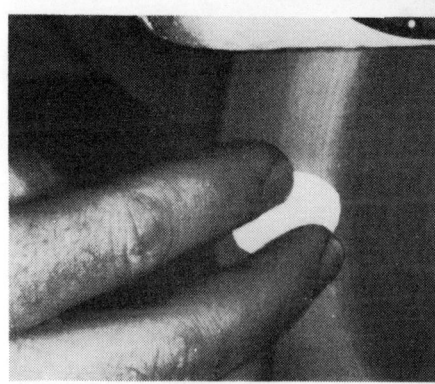

Finish the underside of the stone by hand lapping on a piece of glass with 400 grit. For the best color effect in a doublet, the stone should be quite thin. Some cutters make them as thin as 1 to 3 millimeters.

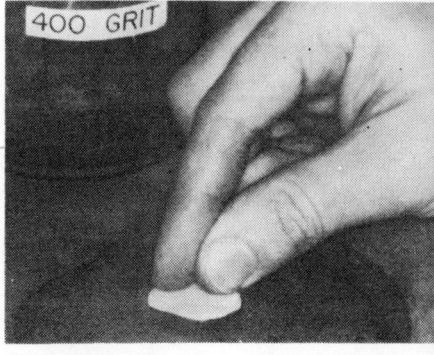

11 — ADVANCED CABOCHON CUTTING

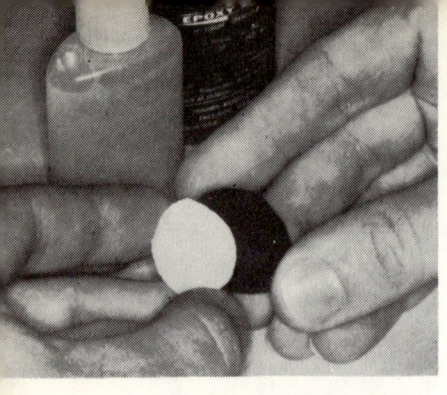

The backing for the opal doublet may be either common (potch) opal, obsidian, black structural glass (obtainable from glass suppliers), or black jade. The first three are easiest to use because their hardness is the same or nearly the same as the opal. Cut a piece a little larger than the gem is to be, and flat lap one surface with 200 and 400 grit. Check the combined thickness of the opal top and the backing with the height of the mounting in which you will set the gem. If it is too thick, grind away some of the bottom of the backing stone. Cement the lapped surfaces of the two stones together.

When the cement has set, cut the assembled gem to the desired size and shape, using your regular cabochon cutting technique. If the stone is small, dop on the top, and grind the bottom to the outline. If the bottom is too thick, grind it to the proper thickness for the mounting in which you will set the stone. Bezel settings are normally used to conceal the assembly. Cut the gem so that the top of the bezel will come above the junction of the stones. Finish the back, and re-dop to cut the top. Grind the top to a low, almost flat crown, smooth, and polish. (Note: it is common practice to cut doublets as double cabochons.)

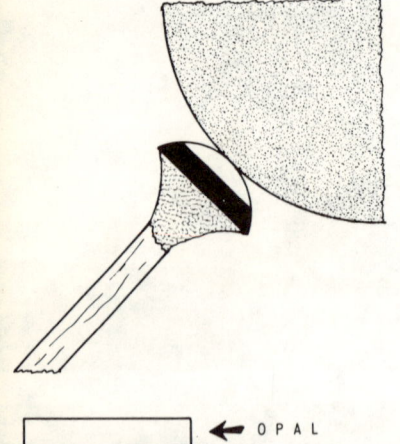

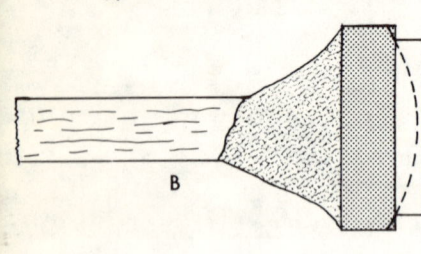

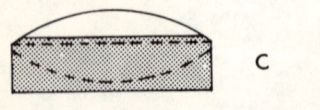

An alternate method of making opal doublets requires a thin piece of opal and a piece of backing material a little larger than the size the finished gem will be. Lap the joining surfaces of the two pieces and cement as shown in drawing A. The assembly is dopped on the bottom and the top cut to the outline shown in drawing B. This will leave a narrow skirt of backing material. The size of the cemented stones will determine the size of the completed gem. Grind carefully so that the skirt around the opal is even. Smooth and polish the top. Re-dop to shape and finish the bottom. The bottom is rounded to make a double cabochon as shown in drawing C. Drawing D is an end view.

Another form of doublet is assembled from a piece of gem material and a protective cap of clear, hard material. Thin pieces of opal are commonly cemented to pieces of clear quartz. As usual, both the cemented surfaces should be previously lapped through 400 grit. Then the assembly is shaped to a regular, flat backed cabochon. Today many rock shops supply finished clear quartz cabochons for this purpose. It makes the job much easier.

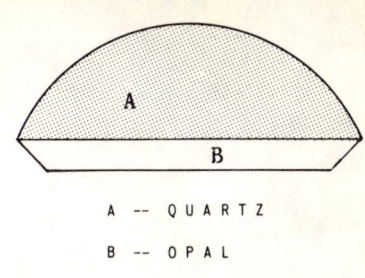

A -- QUARTZ
B -- OPAL

An interesting effect is accomplished by cementing a thin piece of abalone shell to the underside of a piece of clear, black obsidian. Apache tears are ideal for the cap. Then cut a cabochon from the assembly. The rounded top magnifies and reflects the color and pattern of the backing material. (Note: abalone shell should always be ground and sanded wet. When it is worked dry, it releases poisonous fumes that cause nausea. It's safest to cut the shell to the approximate size with a hack saw and lap by hand.)

Triplets

The most common form of triplet is made from a protective cap of clear, hard stone, a thin piece of gem material, and an opaque, dark backing. Triplets with quartz caps, a piece of opal or abalone shell, and an obsidian backing make beautiful gems. To make an opal triplet, lap one surface of a piece of opal to the most attractive color band. Lap the underside of the capping material and cement the two stones together.

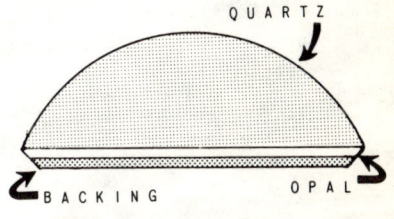

QUARTZ
BACKING   OPAL

When the cement has hardened, lap the opal on the bottom until it is paper thin. The thinner you make the opal, the more brilliant will be the colors. If the opal is already quite thin, it is best to lap entirely by hand, first with 220 grit, then with 400. If it is fairly thick, it can first be carefully ground with a fine grit grinding wheel. Be careful not to grind away too much material.

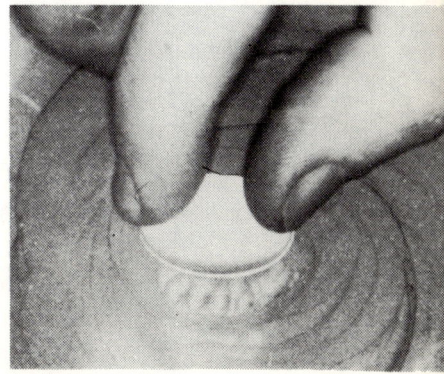

13 — ADVANCED CABOCHON CUTTING

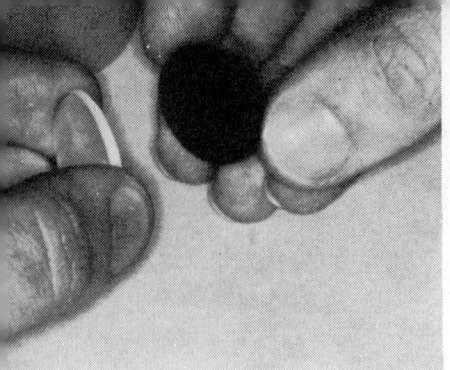

Trim a piece of black obsidian or structural glass to the approximate size the finished gem will be. If this material is fairly thick, grind away some of the undersurface. Then lap the upper surface and cement it to the back of the opal. Let set until the cement hardens completely.

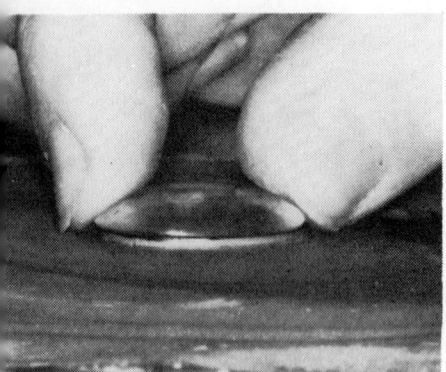

This type of triplet looks best when set in a bezel mounting. The backing must be thin enough to permit the top of the bezel to come over the edge of the quartz cap. If the obsidian is not thin enough, lap it to the proper thickness. If you have a precut quartz cap, the gem is ready to set. If you have used a rough piece of quartz, cut the assembly to a regular, flat-backed cabochon.

Obsidian Doublets and Triplets

Intriguing doublets and triplets may be made from banded obsidian. Select material that is transparent or semitransparent with good banded patterns.

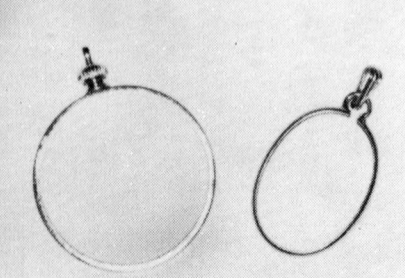

The effectiveness of this gem depends on transmitted light. Therefore, it should be set in a mounting with an open front and back. Cinch mountings are ideal. Another type of setting that can be employed is a mounting made for displaying coins. Coin mountings come in various sizes for different denominations. They are tightened with a screw at the top of the rim.

ADVANCED CABOCHON CUTTING — 14

To make an obsidian doublet, first mark the outline of the chosen gemstone shape on a piece of banded material. Two outlines should be made. If the stone is to be oblong, mark one outline with the bands running lengthwise, and the other with the bands running crosswise. Trim out the two preforms, and lap one surface of each through 400 grit. Both pieces may be lapped at the same time by dopping them to a block of wood. After lapping, cement the two pieces together with the bands running perpendicular to each other.

When the cement has set, grind almost to the gem's outline. Grind the edge perpendicular to the faces of the assembly. The process is the same as cutting a double cabochon (see section on special cabochon shapes). Determine how thick the edge of the cabochon must be to fit the mounting. With an aluminum wire, make marks on either side of the center of the assembly that will be the same distance apart as the necessary thickness.

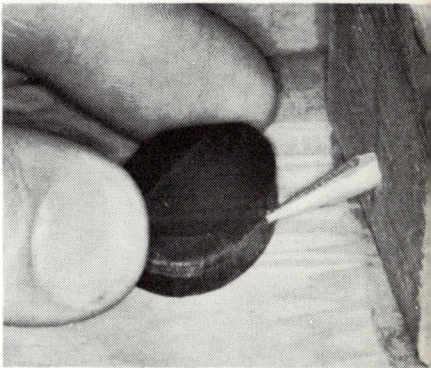

Dop the assembly and grind one surface to a low dome. The edge of the dome should reach the mark. Smooth and polish this surface, and remove the gem from the dop stick. Re-dop and finish the other side.

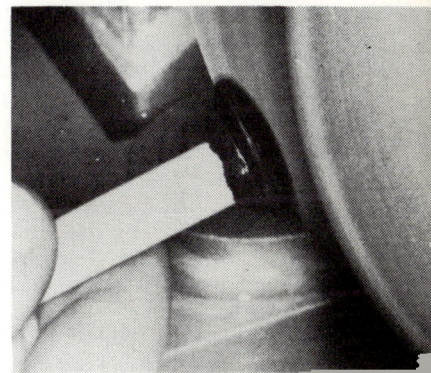

To make an obsidian triplet, mark three cabochon outlines on banded material so that the bands will run at about 120 degrees to each other. Lap one surface of each of these stones through 400 grit. Then cement two of the pieces together. Determine which of the cemented pieces will be on the outside, and which will be in the middle. Then grind and lap the middle piece until it is as thin as possible. It need only be thick enough to retain the pattern. When lapping is completed, cement the third stone to the other surface of the middle stone. Then cut the assembly into a double cabochon.

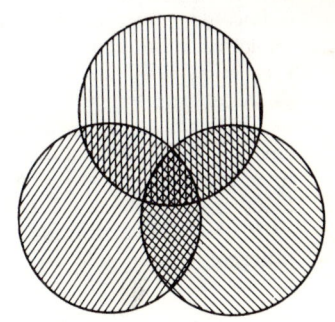

15 — ADVANCED CABOCHON CUTTING

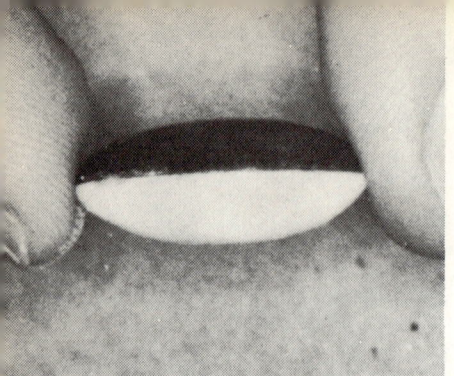

Other Assembled Stones

Two materials of different color may be cemented together and cut as a double cabochon. When this assembly is mounted in a cinch mounting, it can be worn with the side exposed that compliments the wearer's apparel.

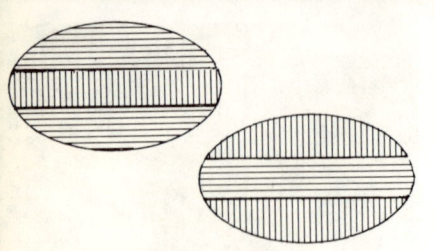

An assembled stone with an unusual effect can be made from three pieces of tigereye. Cement the three pieces together so that the chatoyant bands of one piece run perpendicular to those of the next piece. Cabochons are then cut from these assemblies. Viewed from the top, the cabochons will look like the drawings.

Helpful Hints

Doublets and triplets, especially those made with thin pieces of opal can be quite sensitive to heat. To avoid fracturing, the assembled gem can be dopped by placing it in warm water, and bringing the water to a boil. When it boils, remove the stone, dry it, and dop. Cold dopping techniques as outlined in the dopping section also work well. Avoid heat in smoothing and polishing. To remove an assembled stone dopped with wax, place it in a glass of ice water. If it is warm from polishing, cool it to at least room temperature first.

Some gem cutting experts can cut doublets and triplets so well that the joining line does not show. These can be mounted in any type of setting including prong mountings. If the joining line shows, the stones should be set in a bezel mounting. Settings with soft bezels are preferable because there is less danger of fracturing the gem. If a cast mounting with a heavy bezel is used, set carefully.

Although opal was mentioned extensively in the instructions for making doublets and triplets, any stone worth cutting may be used. Protective caps are especially good for soft stones and gems with pronounced cleavage. By applying this technique many attractive stones may be worn that would be too fragile if they were not protected.

Faceted stones as well as cabochons are sometimes cut as doublets or triplets. A popular gem is composed of a synthetic sapphire top and a synthetic rutile pavilion (bottom). The rutile adds brilliance and life to the stone. Simulated emerald is made from two pieces of clear quartz or synthetic spinel between which is a layer of colored plastic or cement. One of the most common faceted doublets consists of a garnet cap fused to a piece of colored glass. For a unique effect, one hobbyist cemented together two pieces of different colored stone and faceted the assembly with the seam running vertically. The finished stone displayed two different colors side by side.

ADVANCED CABOCHON CUTTING — 16

Gems & Minerals

GEM CUTTER'S HANDBOOK
CAT'S-EYE AND STAR STONES
How To Orient Them

Phenomenal stones, those which produce an attractive optical effect, are popular with gem lovers. The play of color in opal; stars in ruby, sapphire, and garnet; sparkles of light in man-made goldstone; and the billowy light on precious moonstone are examples of gemstone phenomena.

Stones exhibiting phenomena resembling cat's-eyes and stars are very attractive, but many amateurs hesitate to cut these gems because they do not know how to orient them properly. If the stone is oriented and cut correctly, the eye or star will be seen in the exact center of the gem.

Orientation is not difficult if a few techniques developed by experienced and professional cutters are employed. It takes longer to cut a cat's-eye or star stone than a solid-colored gem which requires no orienting. But, when you have finished a beautiful gem with a striking phenomenon in just the right place, it is well worth the time.

What Causes Cat's-eyes

Chatoyancy, the phenomenon that produces a cat's-eye effect can be observed on a spool of thread. Hold the spool under a strong light and you will see a band of light running across it at right angles to the threads. In some gemstones, there are needle-like inclusions of some mineral or minute tubes, all oriented in one direction. If a cabochon is cut from this material so that the inclusions are parallel to the base, a band of light resembling a cat's-eye will run across the crown of the gem at right angles to the inclusions. As the stone is turned at different angles, the eye will move.

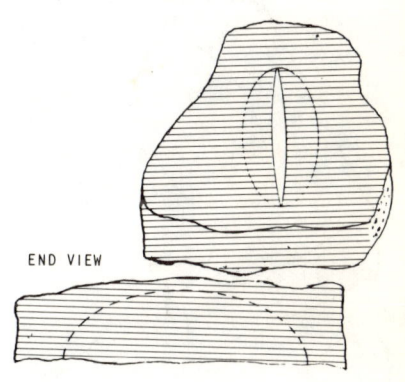
END VIEW

Orienting Tigereye

Tigereye, a gem in which quartz has replaced asbestos fibers, can be cut into attractive cat's-eye stones. To produce a good eye, the fibers must be fine and as straight as possible. It is very important to cut slabs of tigereye so that they are oriented correctly. The slabs must be sawed so that their surfaces are parallel to the plane of the fibers. This may require that the rough stone be clamped at an angle in the saw vise. (See sections on slab sawing.)

CORRECT

EDGE VIEW OF SLABS

INCORRECT

17 — ADVANCED CABOCHON CUTTING

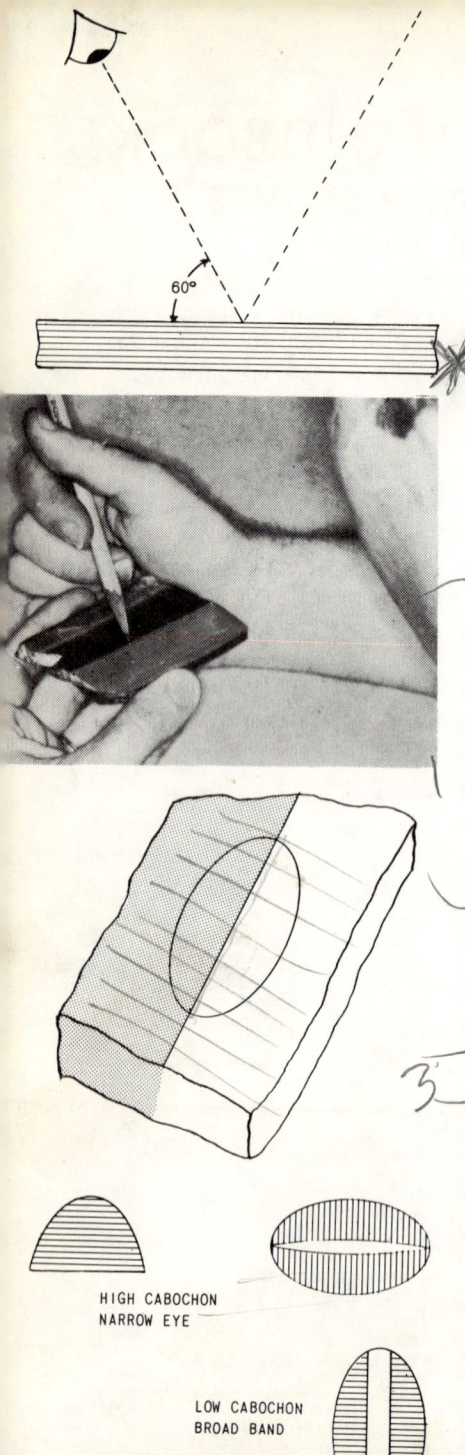

Hold the slab parallel to the floor with the fibers running toward you. Now look across its surface at an angle of 60 degrees. The half of the surface closest to you should be either dark or light. The half farthest from you should be the opposite (i.e., if the half nearest you is light, the other half should be dark).

Make a light pencil mark at the dividing line between the light and dark halves.

Holding the slab with the base in the same plane, rotate it 180 degrees so that the halves are reversed. Again look across the surface at 60 degrees. The light and dark areas should be in the same positions as they were before the slab was rotated. If the half nearest you was light, it should still be light after rotating. Once more, mark the dividing line between the dark and light areas. If the stone was slabbed properly, the two pencil marks will coincide. Now turn the slab over to expose the underside. The light and dark areas should reverse themselves. If the half toward you on the other surface was light, the half toward you now should be dark. The surface on which the light side is toward you should be the base. Mark the outline of the gem on this side, and cut it as a cabochon. If you are cutting an oval stone, place the outline so that the dividing line runs along the long axis of the oval. For a narrow eye, cut a high cabochon. A medium or low cabochon produces a broad band of light. *Note: These instructions presuppose that the fibers extend entirely across the slab. Sometimes slabs of tigereye contain dark opaque areas that exhibit no fibers or chatoyance. In this case, use only that portion of the slab in which you can see the fibers.*

HIGH CABOCHON
NARROW EYE

LOW CABOCHON
BROAD BAND

ADVANCED CABOCHON CUTTING — 18

Other Tigereye Cuts

For a cab that exhibits an unusual jumping flash instead of a centrally located eye, try using the surface on which the dark area was toward you for a base. Mark an outline for an oval stone so that the long axis of the stone will be at about 45 degrees to the dividing line between the light and dark areas. The cabochon may be cut medium, medium high, or high. The height at which it is cut will vary the width of the flash. By varying the angle of the long axis to the dividing line between light and dark areas, different effects will be produced.

Another novel effect **requires a good** piece of close, straight-grained tigereye. Saw a thick slab parallel to the plane of the eyes (perpendicular to the fibers). Cut a high crowned, round cabochon from the slab to produce a bull's-eye effect of alternating light and dark bands. This cut requires good material and skill.

Orienting Other Cat's-eye Stones

Tourmaline, beryl and a host of other gemstones may have inclusions that will cause cat's-eyes. In most cases, the inclusions are visible to the naked eye. To check a piece of rough gem material, coat it with light oil and hold it under a single source of strong white light. Direct sunlight is ideal. The best artificial light is an unfrosted incandescent bulb. Rotate the gem and check all sides for a bright sheen which moves back and forth across the surface. If you locate this sheen (chatoyancy), try to distinguish the inclusions. In some rare instances, magnification may be needed. The inclusions, sometimes referred to as silk, should be fine, parallel, and running in one direction to produce a good eye.

Cut the base of the stone parallel to the inclusions. If you plan to cut an eliptical gem, the inclusions should run parallel to the short axis if at all possible so that the eye will be parallel to the long axis. Stones such as tourmaline are often found as crystals or crystal fragments. The prism faces of these crystals are parallel to the silk. Therefore, a prism face can be used as a base, making orientation a simple chore.

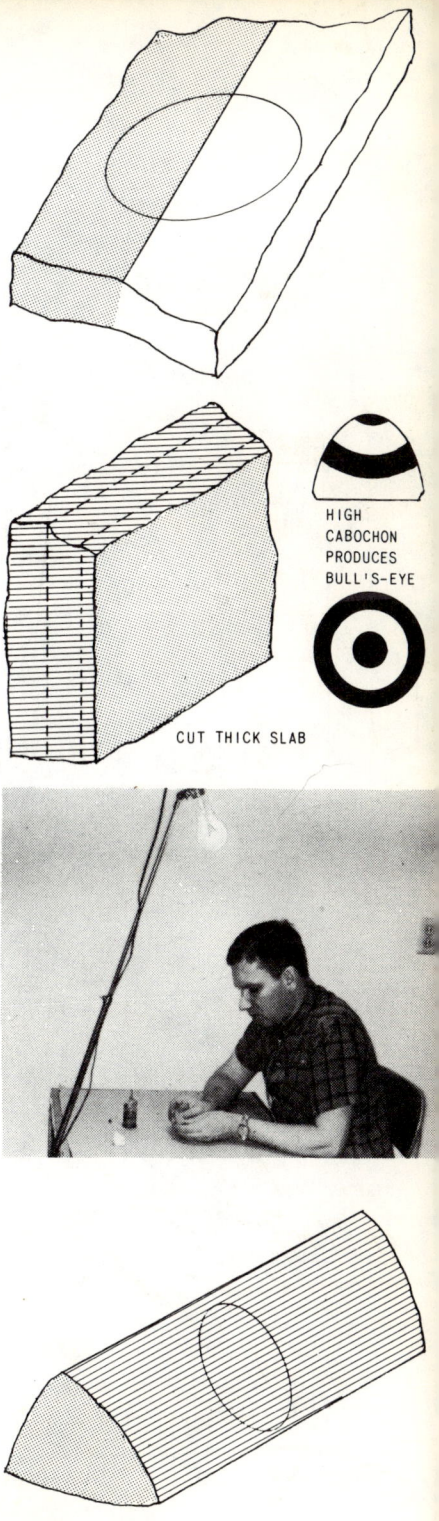

HIGH CABOCHON PRODUCES BULL'S-EYE

CUT THICK SLAB

19 — ADVANCED CABOCHON CUTTING

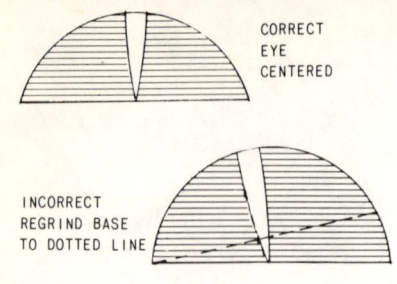

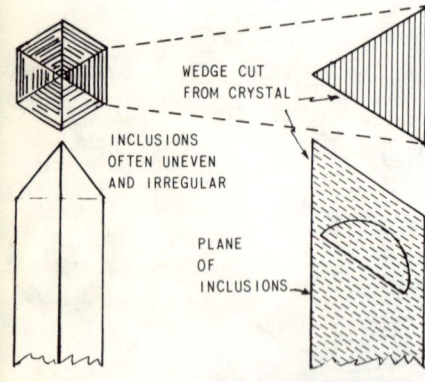

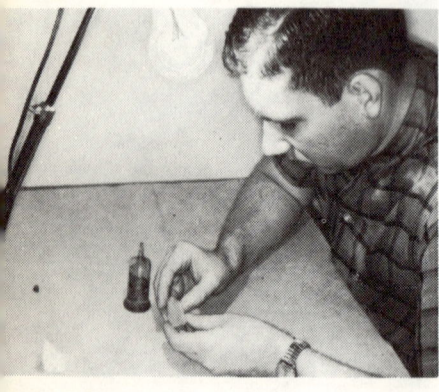

After you have cut a base parallel to the fibers, cut the other side into a domed cabochon. If the base is oriented correctly, there will be a narrow eye in the center of the dome. To check this, oil the stone and hold it under a single source of strong white light. It may be necessary to smooth the cabochon and possibly bring it to a semi-polish. If the eye is off center, the base should be reground to orient it. Do not try to center by re-grinding the crown unless the crown is not symmetrical. When the eye is centered, smooth and polish the stone.

Cat's-eye Quartz

There is some white crystalline quartz which has fine tubular inclusions that run parallel to the faces of the crystal terminations, not the prism faces. These inclusions are often distorted and unevenly distributed. Gems of this material must be cut so that their bases will be parallel to one of the termination faces. They must also be cut from pie-shaped sections no larger than the termination faces. Some cutters actually saw the crystal lengthwise into pie-shaped wedges which correspond to the termination faces (see diagram).

Orienting Moonstone for Cat's-eyes

A different method is needed to orient moonstone; except for the high-quality material from India, it does not contain fibers. The sheen, adularescence, is generally attributed to reflections from included layers of kaolin. White, green, and many other colors of moonstone are available.

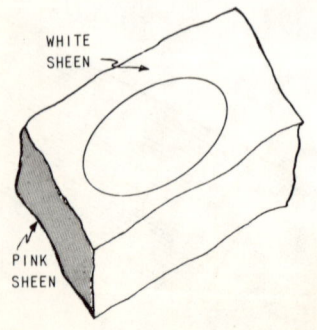

To cut the white variety, oil the rough gem and hold it directly under a single unfrosted bulb. Move your head in toward the stone until the light beam just grazes your forehead. Turn the stone in different directions until you locate a strong white sheen. Then look for a fainter pink sheen. The base of the gem should be cut parallel to the white sheen and at right angles to the pink.

ADVANCED CABOCHON CUTTING — 20

After the base has been cut, hold the stone base down under the light with the base parallel to the floor. Move your head close to the light beam as you did before, and see if the sheen is visible. If you must tilt the stone to observe the sheen, the eye will be off center. To remedy this, re-grind the base to make it parallel to the sheen. Grind until the sheen is visible without tilting the gem. Do not try to orient by grinding the top.

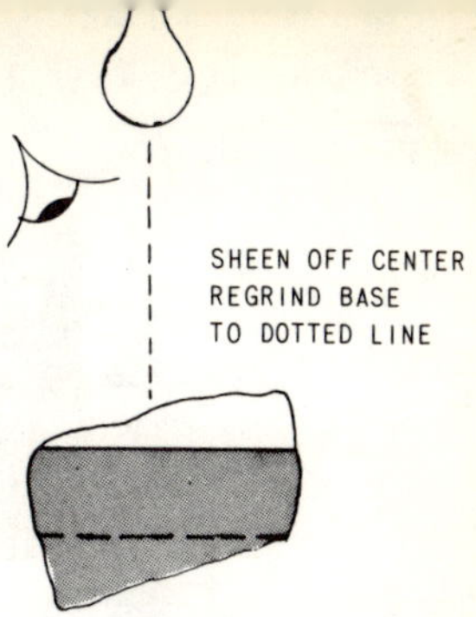

Another method to determine if the base is properly oriented is to hold the stone with the base up and parallel to the floor. With the base in this position, rotate the stone a full 360 degrees. If the sheen extends entirely across the base throughout the complete rotation, it is properly oriented. If at any point, you have to tip the base to observe the sheen, more orientation grinding is necessary.

If you plan to cut an elongated stone, the eye should run parallel to the long axis. The long axis should therefore be perpendicular to the pink sheen. Another way to determine the direction in which the eye will run is to observe the cleavage planes normally found on moonstone. The eye will run perpendicular to these planes.

Orienting Colored Moonstone

Colored moonstone is oriented much the same as the white variety. Observe it under an unfrosted light, but this time look for a strong silvery, slightly yellowish sheen. If you cut the stone with the base parallel to this sheen, you will have a gem with a billowy light which runs across its surface (many moonstones are cut this way), but there will be no cat's-eye. To orient for the eye, turn the stone until you locate a bluish sheen which is not so pronounced as the other. Cut the base parallel to this bluish adularescence. The eye will be perpendicular to the yellowish sheen and at right angles to any cleavage planes. *Note: On both white and colored moonstones there are usually striations on the faces which produce the eyes — another orientation check.*

21 — ADVANCED CABOCHON CUTTING

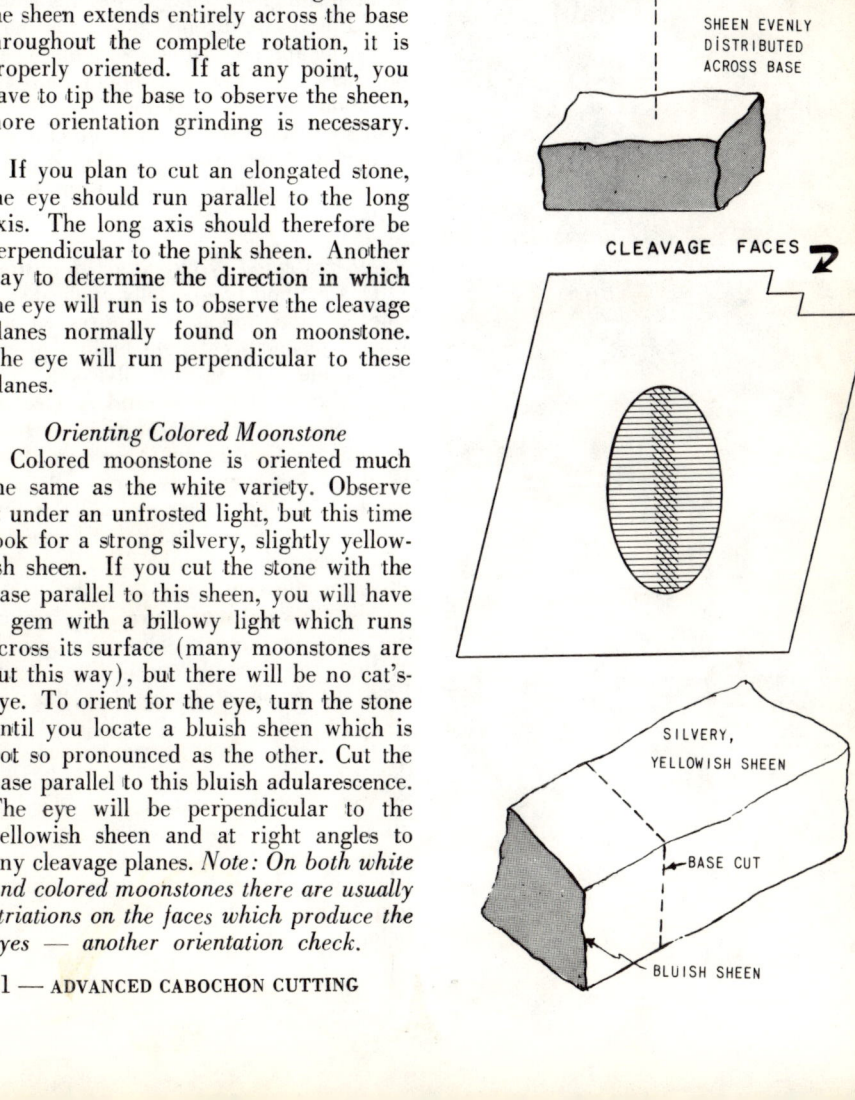

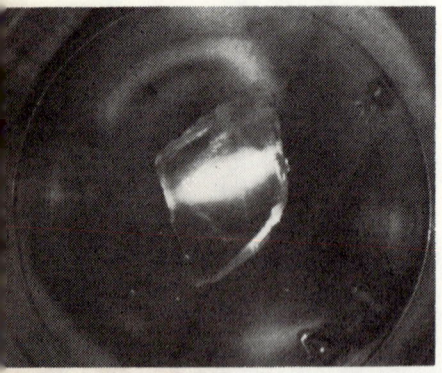

There is a foolproof method of locating the direction of the eye on moonstone, using a light and immersion fluid. Don't try this until the base is in absolutely perfect alignment with the sheen. Considering the refractive index of moonstone, you can use ordinary linseed oil, anise oil, cinnamon oil, or glycerine as an immersion fluid. Put an electric bulb in a tin can or lightproof box with a small 1/16-inch hole drilled over the light bulb. Use a small glass jar on the can or box. Center the stone over the hole, and turn on the light. The eye will be visible immediately. Mark the direction on the stone with a pencil and lay out the shape of the cabochon, with the mark forming the long axis of the stone. Use this method only after you have definitely aligned the base with the sheen, otherwise the ray will not follow the mark on the finished stone. This device works well with stones where no cleavage planes or striations are visible. It's also an aid for beginners who want to be sure.

Another Method of Orienting Moonstone

This method is especially applicable to colored moonstone. It requires an unfrosted incandescent light bulb, a pencil, and a piece of ¼-inch plywood. The stone should rest on a solid surface directly under the bulb. Move your head in until the light beam grazes your forehead so that your eyes are as close to the line of light as possible. Turn and twist the moonstone until you locate the silvery-yellowish sheen. Then hold the stone in this position. Rest the pencil on the plywood and move both around the gem, marking a solid line entirely around its circumference. Be sure to keep the stone in position so that the sheen is visible. The line will be parallel to the sheen. Turn the moonstone 90 degrees so that the pencil mark is now on top. Rotate the stone with the line always on top. Somewhere in this plane you will find the lighter, bluish sheen; when you do, hold the stone securely and make a pencil mark as you did before.

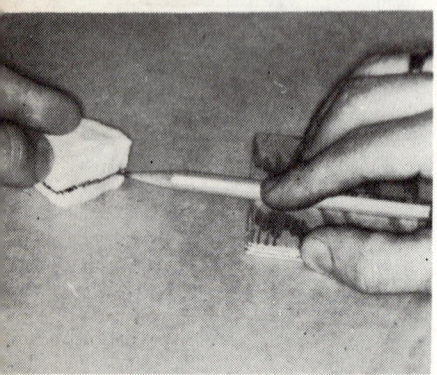

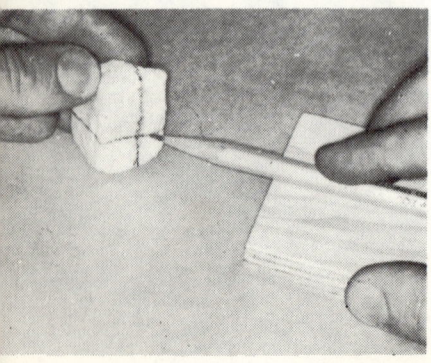

ADVANCED CABOCHON CUTTING — 22

The stone is now marked with two lines at right angles to each other. The base should be cut parallel to the second line (parallel to the bluish sheen). This marking process can also be used to locate and orient the white and pink sheens in white moonstone. Use one of the methods previously described to locate the direction of the eye.

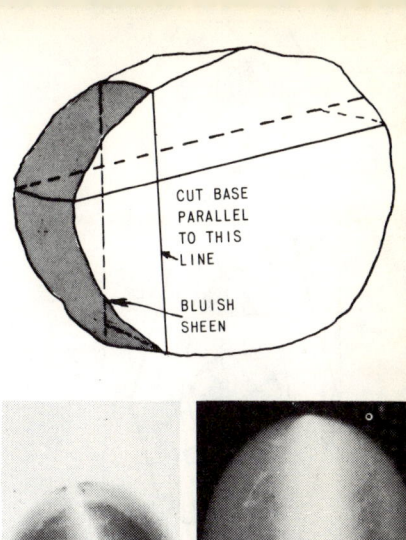

Cat's-eye Gem Shapes

To exhibit an eye, the stone must have a domed surface. A flat surface yields only a flash. Most materials look best when cut as plump, high crowned cabochons. However, because of the shape of the material, it may have to be cut with a low crown. Depending on the material's shape and the cutter's wishes, the stone may be cut as a round, an oval or a navette. The eye should run with the long axis of an elongated stone.

Cat's-eye gems are often cut as double cabochons with high crowns and low domed bases. The base of transparent and translucent gems are frequently left unpolished to prevent light leakage through the back. This is a common practice with chrysoberyl cat's-eyes. *Note: Chrysoberyl is a very hard gem which requires special cutting techniques. These techniques will be reviewed in a subsequent section.*

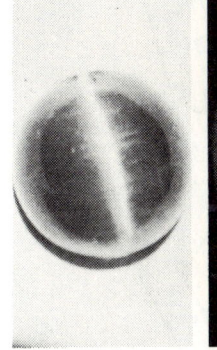
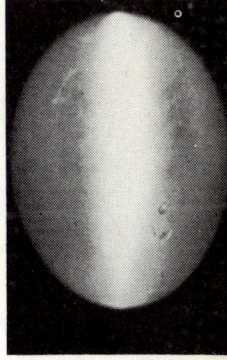

Star Stones

Like cat's-eyes, stars in gems are caused by silk composed of minute tubes or needle-like mineral inclusions. If the inclusions are all parallel in one plane, a cat's-eye will result; if there are several sets of parallel inclusions oriented at different angles to each other, a star is produced. In star ruby, sapphire, and quartz, three sets of inclusions oriented at 60 degrees produce six-rayed stars. In star garnet, there are groups of inclusions that parallel the edges of the rhombic faces of the rhombic dodecahedron crystals. Star garnets usually exhibit 4-rayed stars. In all star stones, however, there may be freak stars because of variation or imperfection in the inclusions and twinned crystals; 4, 5, 6, 7, and up to 12-rayed stars have been found.

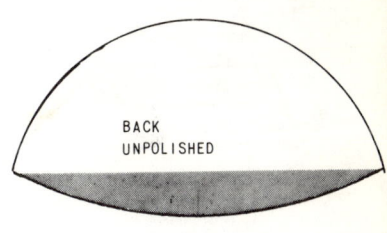

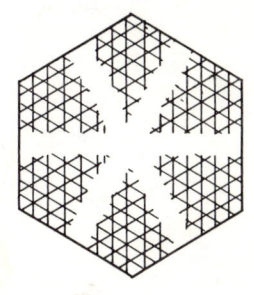

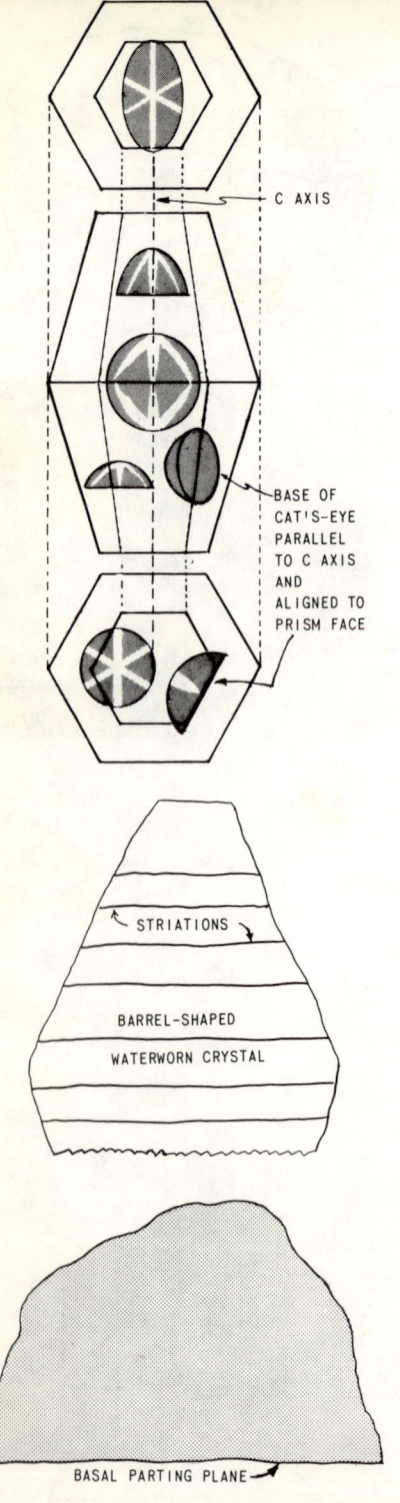

In stones which crystallize in the hexagonal system, such as ruby, sapphire and quartz, the inclusions are oriented at right angles to the long axis of the crystal. This invisible axis, known as the C axis, plays a very important part in orienting the star. A star stone must be cut with its base perpendicular to the C axis.

Rubies and blue sapphires are commonly found as whole or broken crystals. As the drawing illustrates, a long crystal will yield several star stones. Spheres cut from this material would exhibit two stars. If a cabochon is cut with its base parallel to the C axis, it will produce a cat's-eye. *Note: The cat's-eye stone must also be in alignment with a prism face as shown in the drawing.*

The crystal faces of rubies and blue sapphires often show striations which are helpful in orienting the base of the gem. These striations are approximately perpendicular to the C axis. If the crystal is long enough, you can saw several small slabs. To save material, a faceter's trim saw with a thin blade should be used if available (see section on trim sawing). Saw parallel to the striations.

Black sapphire is usually found in rough, irregular chunks (mostly water worn pebbles) not in crystal form. Therefore, crystal faces cannot be used as an orienting aid. However, on most pebbles there is a flat or slightly concave basal parting plane which is perpendicular to the C axis. This parting plane can be used for a base.

Basal partings and striations are helpful in orienting the base of a star stone, but usually more orientation is necessary to get the star perfectly centered. The next section of *Gem Cutter's Handbook* will describe several methods and tools which will help you orient a stone to exhibit a perfect star.

ADVANCED CABOCHON CUTTING — 24

Gems & Minerals

GEM CUTTER'S HANDBOOK
CAT'S-EYE AND STAR STONES
Orienting — Part 2

The previous section covered the orienting of cat's-eye gems and a few pointers on orienting asteriated (star) stones. In this section, several methods of orienting star stones, and some helpful hints are reviewed.

At the end of the section is a list of stones that may produce cat's-eyes and stars. Some of the favorite star materials are ruby, sapphire, garnet, and quartz. Do not expect to find a star in every piece. Only those that have the necessary inclusions will be asteriated.

Only general cutting techniques are given in this section. The next section will cover the specific techniques for cutting hard materials such as ruby, sapphire, and chrysoberyl in detail.

Stars in Ruby and Blue Sapphire

Asteriated stones from these materials are usually opaque or only slightly translucent. The first step in orienting is to check for chatoyancy. Oil the stone and hold it under a strong white light (see previous section). When you have located a chatoyant area, saw or grind a base, trying to make it parallel to the plane of chatoyancy. If the stone exhibits any of the striations mentioned in the previous section, use these as a cutting aid. If you have a long crystal, you may be able to cut several small slabs from it. Next grind a rounded top on the gem. It is not necessary to grind a perfect cabochon shape, just so it is domed. However, it may be necessary to smooth the stone and even give it a semipolish. When this is done, oil the dome and lay the stone, base down, on a horizontal flat surface directly under a strong, unfrosted, white light bulb. Move your head in until the light beam just grazes the forehead. Again locate the chatoyancy. Mark the center of the chatoyant area with a pencil. *Note: several brands of immersion oil that are excellent for locating chatoyancy are available from rock shops and catalog suppliers. Refer to current rockhound magazine advertisements.*

— ADVANCED CABOCHON CUTTING

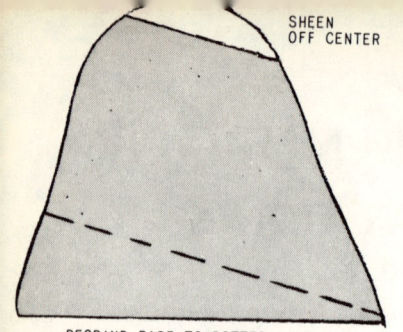

REGRIND BASE TO DOTTED LINE

SHEEN OFF CENTER

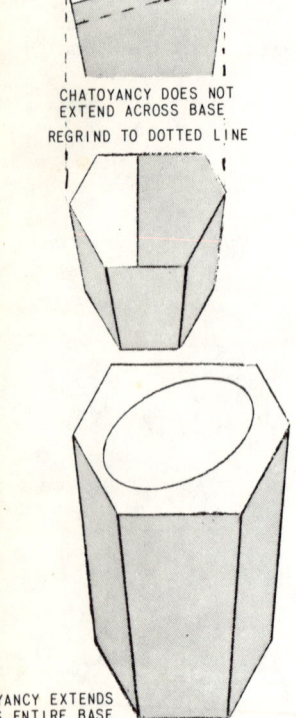

CHATOYANCY DOES NOT EXTEND ACROSS BASE
REGRIND TO DOTTED LINE

CHATOYANCY EXTENDS ACROSS ENTIRE BASE

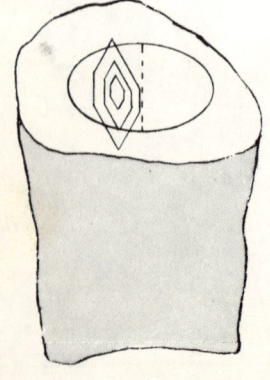

If the pencil mark is in the center of the dome, the stone is properly oriented. Most of the time the mark will not be centered. If this is the case, the base must be re-ground so that it will be parallel to the chatoyancy. Grind slowly and carefully so that you do not waste material. Stop frequently to oil the dome and check under the light. When you can set the base on a horizontal surface under the light and observe the chatoyancy to be well-centered, you are ready to cut the stone into a cabochon. *Note: always orient the chatoyancy by grinding the base; it is almost impossible to orient by grinding the top.*

An Alternate Method

Instead of orienting from the top, some experts prefer to check the chatoyancy in the base of the gem. The chatoyancy is located, and an attempt made to saw or grind a base parallel to it. After the base is cut, the stone is held under a strong white light with the base parallel to the floor. The head is moved in as usual, and the chatoyancy observed to see if it extends across the entire base. Often you will have to tilt the stone to see the chatoyancy. If so, more grinding is needed. The chatoyancy must extend across the entire base, even when the stone is rotated 180 degrees with the base in the same plane. If it does not, regrind according to the paragraph above. When this is accomplished, mark the gem's shape on the base and rough out the cabochon. Before finishing the cabochon, it is a good idea to check the top to make sure the chatoyancy is centered. *Note: to guarantee correct orientation, you can combine the two orienting methods just described.*

In most rubies and blue sapphires, you will find zoning lines on the bases which parallel the sides of the crystal. If you are planning to cut an oval, mark the outline so that the short axis of the oval parallels one of these lines. This will orient the star so that one ray runs the length of the stone.

ADVANCED CABOCHON CUTTING — 26

Black Star Sapphire

Black star sapphire is found as waterworn pebbles, and the crystal faces are seldom evident. If there is a basal parting, you can use it as an orienting aid by cutting the base parallel to it (see previous section). Then use either the chatoyancy at the top or bottom, or both, to orient the base. If there is no basal parting evident, oil the stone and look for chatoyancy. Mark the chatoyancy with a pencil and proceed to cut a base parallel to it.

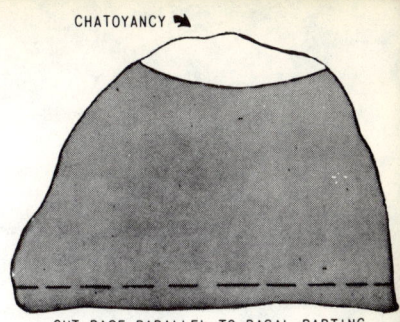

CUT BASE PARALLEL TO BASAL PARTING

Orienting Star Garnet

The best star garnets are translucent, not clear. The stars are found on the centers of the rhombic faces of the garnet's rhombic dodecahedron crystals. A complete crystal can produce as many as 12 stars. However, most garnets are found as waterworn pebbles. Often wedge-shaped stones are found. In most cases the apex of the wedge was once the center of a rhombic crystal face.

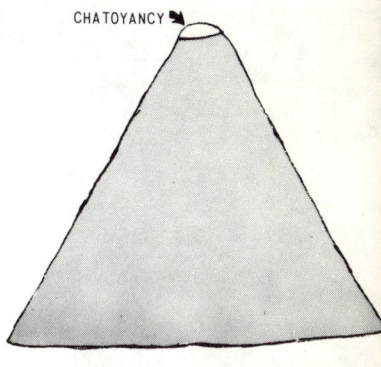

Grind a dome on the apex and smooth it. Oil the dome and hold the stone under a strong light with your head in the usual observation position. Twist and turn the stone until you locate one ray of the star. Hold the stone so that this remains visible and tip the top until the other ray comes into view. Turn the garnet until the rays intersect at their centers and the intersection is directly below the light. Mark this spot. Grind a base so that the intersection of the rays will be centered in the top.

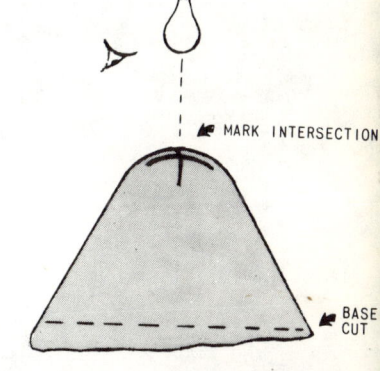

A much better method to locate pieces of garnets with stars is to tumble-polish them. If you do not have enough garnets for a tumbler load and must add other stones, be sure the other stones are of the same hardness. Follow the manufacturer's instructions on tumbling. If you do not have a tumbler, tumble polished star garnets are available from various gem and mineral suppliers. All that is necessary is to locate a star and cut the tumbled gem so that the star is centered on the top.

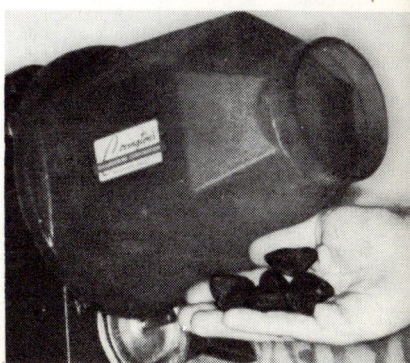

27 — **ADVANCED CABOCHON CUTTING**

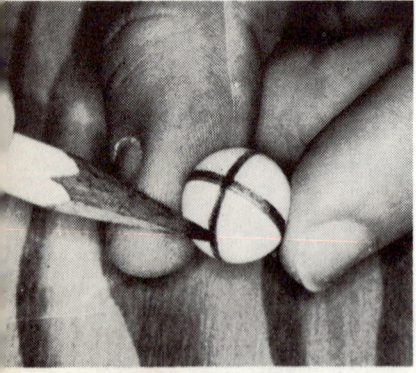

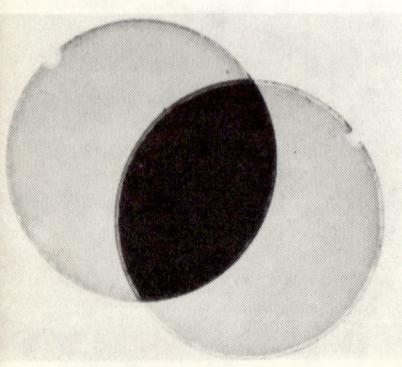

Orienting Star Quartz

Rose quartz is a favorite star material. To determine if a piece of quartz is asteriated, use the same lighting device that is used to locate the direction of eyes in cat's-eye stones (see previous section). Immerse the stone and center it over the pinpoint of light. A commercial immersion fluid with about the same refractive index as quartz (available from rock hobby suppliers) is recommended. Turn the stone in all directions. If it is asteriated, a star will appear. If the exterior of the stone is rough, you may have to grind and smooth it first. Of course, the gem must be translucent if the light is to be used.

To orient the star, you can cut the stone into a sphere (sphere cutting is covered in the Handbook, *Specialized Gem Cutting*). Immerse the sphere over the light. You will find two stars at opposite ends of the C axis. Draw a line completely around the sphere connecting the two stars. Then draw another line at right angles to the first line. Dop the sphere to a block of wood with the first line perpendicular to the block. Clamp the block in a saw vise and saw parallel to the second line to make two star stones with the stars correctly oriented. The sphere method can also be used on other star gems. On opaque materials you will probably have to polish the sphere to locate the stars. This method is not recommended for expensive gems because it wastes material.

Instead of cutting the quartz into a sphere you can locate the C axis with a polariscope, a gem testing instrument. If you cut a base perpendicular to the C axis, the star will be properly oriented. The polariscope is built around two polaroid discs. These discs filter light rays so that the rays vibrate in one direction only. If you hold the two discs together in front of a light and rotate one disc, the light passing through will grow dimmer and dimmer until it is extinguished. This is referred to as "crossed polaroids."

ADVANCED CABOCHON CUTTING — 28

Ready-made polariscopes are available or you can build your own. This one is made from:

2 — polarizing filters about 2 inches in diameter
2 — drain pipe wall flanges (escutcheons) for 1½ inch pipe
1 — tin can to fit the pipe flanges. A dog food can is just the right size.
1 — standard light socket
1 — 7½ to 25 watt lamp
1 — standard plug and cord
2 — machine screws about 1½ inches long, with nuts
1 — pc. plywood 3¼x3¾x⅜ inches
1 — pc. wood 4x4x¾ inches
1 — pc. wood 1¼x11½x⅜ inches
Wood screws, washers, and glue

The polaroid discs are available from Edmund Scientific Co., Barrington, N.J., for a nominal price. The other materials can be found at hardware stores and lumber yards.

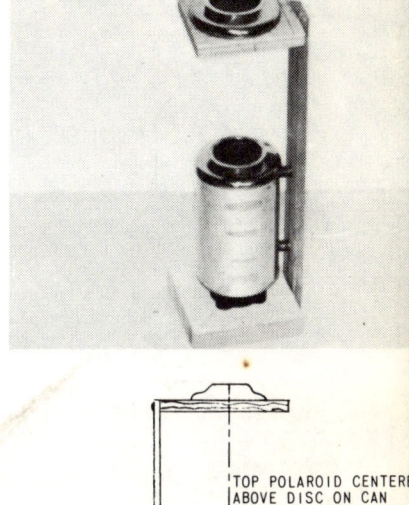

The polaroids are held in the flanges with Scotch tape. Assemble the socket, cord and plug. Screw the socket to the 4x4 piece of wood so that it is well centered. Screw and glue the long strip of wood to the 4x4. Attach the can to the long strip with the 1½-inch bolts and nuts. Use washers to space so that the can is centered over the light. Press a flange with a disc on the can. The ⅜-inch plywood is screwed and glued to the top of the wood strip. Before mounting, a 2-inch hole is cut in the plywood which must center over the polaroid in the can.

The other polaroid disc in its flange is held in position by three small wood screws under each of which are three small washers. These can be adjusted so the flange is centered, but still free to rotate to bring the polaroid discs into crossed position. *Note: Dimensions and materials listed are not critical. The important ingredients are a light source, one disc centered above the other and a means of rotating the upper disc to cross the polaroids.*

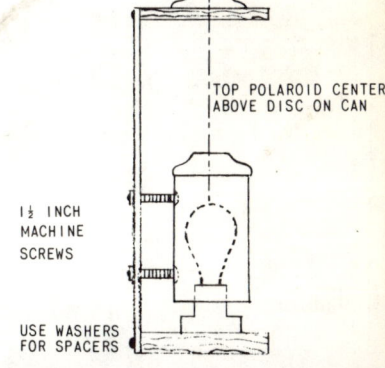

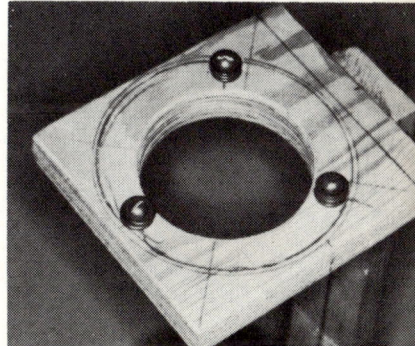

29 — ADVANCED CABOCHON CUTTING

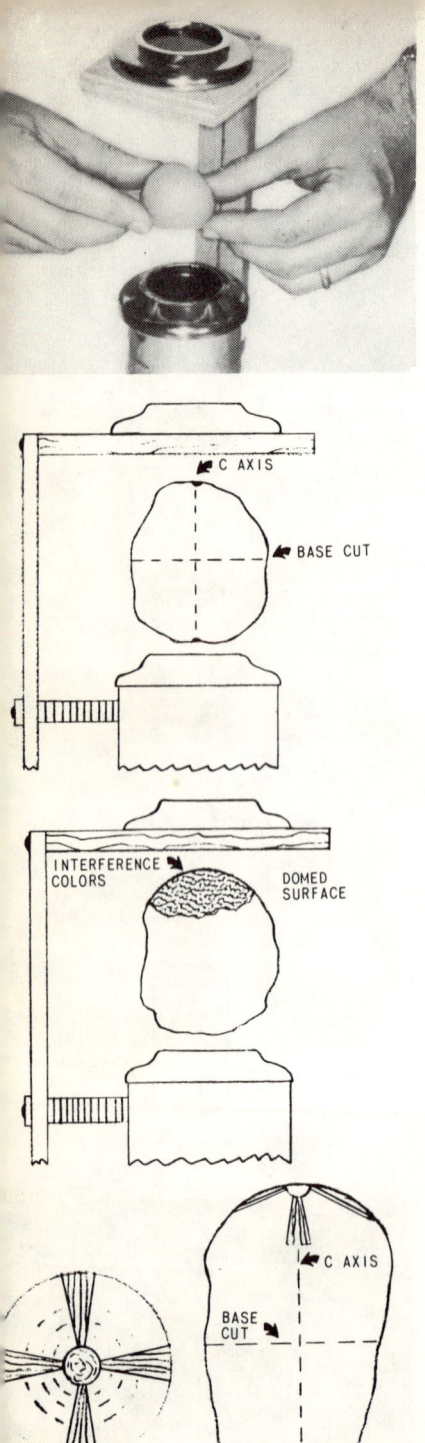

To orient the quartz, turn on the light and look down through the upper disc. Rotate the disc until the light is extinguished. Then hold the quartz between the discs and rotate it. In all but two positions, the quartz will turn light and dark every time it is rotated 90 degrees. The only time it does not do this is when you look through it along the C axis. When you find a position in which it does not turn light and dark, make a mark on the top of the stone. Then turn the quartz bottom side up and rotate again. Mark this surface at the position where the stone does not turn light and dark during rotation. If a base is cut perpendicular to an imaginary line between the two marks, the base should be at right angles to the C axis. *Note: gems tested under a polariscope must be translucent. Good star quartz meets this requirement. Before using the polariscope, check the stone for asterism by immersing it over the pinpoint of light.*

An Additional Polariscope Test

This additional test will help you to positively locate the C axis. After making the test just outlined, grind and smooth a dome on the quartz at one of the ends you have marked. Oil the dome and hold the stone between crossed polaroids. Turn and twist the stone until you note a patch of brilliant colors. These "interference colors" indicate that you are near the C axis. To locate the exact position of the star, you must find an interference figure. After the interference colors are noted, just a little more twisting and turning should make this figure appear on the dome. On quartz the figure looks like the drawing, a set of crossed brushes with a circle in the center. The brushes and circles vary in color in different pieces of material. The center of the circle in the figure will be the center of the star. Mark it. The base should be cut at right angles to an imaginary line (the C axis) running perpendicularly through the center of the figure.

ADVANCED CABOCHON CUTTING — 30

When you have oriented the star, cut the quartz into a cabochon. Most star quartz is too pale to display the star to advantage. To remedy this, the stone can be backed with a colored mirror or a plain mirror cemented to the back of the quartz with colored epoxy. For complete instructions see the section on assembled stones.

Helpful Hints

On some material it is possible to determine if it will produce a star by placing a globule of oil or model cement on a chatoyant area. The globule forms a tiny hemisphere, a miniature cabochon, so to speak. On good star gems, a tiny star will appear on the surface of the globule when it is held under a strong light. Black star sapphire is often tested this way using a globule of Aster-Oil.

MINIATURE STAR APPEARS ON GLOBULE

Star stones are generally cut as rounds or ovals. Ovals should be cut with one ray of the star running parallel to the long axis. Like cat's-eye gems, star stones are often cut as double cabochons. Oriental gem cutters frequently cut them with medium to high domes on the back to add to the weight of the stone and increase the price. Often the stars are off center. Sometimes it is possible to buy a stone that was poorly cut in the Orient and recut it into a much better gem. Spheres of star material make good novelty items.

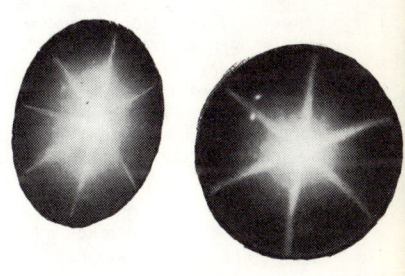

The tubular inclusions in many cat's-eye gems can absorb polishing compounds, and it is virtually impossible to remove it. If the tubes are large enough, you can fill them by immersing the gem in sodium silicate (water glass). More than one immersion may be necessary. Let the sodium silicate harden before cutting. If the tubes will not absorb the sodium silicate, polish the stone on a wet buff; a dry buff drives the polishing compound into the tubes.

31 — ADVANCED CABOCHON CUTTING

More Helpful Hints

Some experts prefer a flashlight for orienting chatoyant gems. The base of the flashlight is pressed against the lips, and the stone placed directly below the light. When a base has been cut on the stone, it is placed on a horizontal surface, base down, and the light held about 12 inches directly above it. The advocates of this method feel that there is less chance of cutting the stone with a star or eye off center.

The polariscope has many uses. For complete information on this instrument and how different materials react to polarized light, refer to a book on gemology (gem identification).

Avoid purchasing chatoyant gem material with laminations, fractures, and unsightly inclusions. Rough material that has been oriented is available from some suppliers. Although prime ruby and sapphire may sell for hundreds or even thousands of dollars per carat, there is good material within a hobbyist's price range.

A common error in orienting ruby and sapphire is mistaking the flashes from platy parting planes for chatoyancy. True chatoyancy glows from within the stone; the flashes are on the surface. On most stones, zoning lines are also apparent when the true chatoyancy is viewed.

If you are cutting expensive material, do not waste it by cutting to a standard size. It is better to cut the largest size possible and have a special mounting made. However, if the material is blemished, it is best to cut a smaller gem and eliminate the imperfections. Whenever possible, cut the base from the widest part of the stone. Star rubies and sapphires are often mounted in cast rings known as "gypsy mountings."

Both tourmaline and garnet chip. Grind carefully on well dressed, smooth wheels. Both stones are fairly heat sensitive — sand wet. Linde A on leather is a good polishing combination for these gems.

Moonstone will cleave. Be sure to grind it on a smooth wheel. It polishes nicely on felt with cerium oxide.

In some stones such as chrysoberyl, the inclusions may be so fine that you cannot locate them. To orient such a gem, oil it and search for chatoyancy. Then cut a base parallel to the plane of the chatoyancy.

As you cut, be sure to check cat's-eye and star stones frequently to make sure the eye or star is centered. The cutting of chrysoberyl, ruby, and sapphire will be covered in the next section.

Any mineral which has the necessary inclusions can produce an eye or a star, but not all specimens of a given mineral will be chatoyant. The most common chatoyant gems are chrysoberyl, garnet, moonstone, quartz, ruby, sapphire, and tourmaline. In other stones like beryl, eyes and stars are not so common, but they are found. Some of the minerals which have produced chatoyant gems are listed below.

Gemstones Which May Produce Cat's-eyes or Stars

E — Stones which produce Cat's-eyes

actinolite E
amozonite E
andalusite E S
anthophyllite E
apatite E S
aragonite E
barite E
beryl
  aquamarine E S
  black S
  bronze E
  emerald E S
  goshenite E
  green E
  heliodor E
  morganite E
  peach E
binghamite E
bronzite E
calcite
  spar E
cassiterite E
celestite E

cerussite E
chrysoberyl E S
  alexandrite
  cat's-eye
clinozoisite E
corundum S E
  ruby
  sapphire
danburite E
diopside E S
enstatite E
epidote E
feldspar
  labradorite E
  moonstone
  albite E
  moonstone
  orthoclase E S
  peristerite E
  sunstone E S
fluorite E
furcronite E
garnet S E

S — Stones which produce stars

goethite E
gypsum
  spar E
hypersthene E
iolite E S
jade E
kornerupine E
kyanite E
malachite E
mesolite E
obsidian E
opal E S
pectolite E
peridot E S
petalite E
pollucite E
prehnite E
quartz
  rose S E
  tigereye E
  white E
rutile E
scapolite E

serpentine E
sillimanite E
sphalerite E
spinel S E
spodumene E
  hiddenite
  kunzite
  triphane
topaz E
tourmaline E S
  achroite
  dravite
  indicolite
  green
  pink
  rubelite
  yellow
tremolite E
ulexite E
willemite E
williamsite E
witherite E
zircon E S

ADVANCED CABOCHON CUTTING — 32

Gems &
Minerals

GEM CUTTER'S HANDBOOK

CAT'S-EYE AND STAR STONES
Part 3 — Cutting Hard Gems

In the previous section, cutting hints were listed for some of the popular cat's-eyes and star stones such as moonstone and garnet. Three popular chatoyant stones, chrysoberyl, ruby, and sapphire, require special techniques. These gems are all extremely hard; chrysoberyl is $8\frac{1}{2}$ on the Mohs scale of hardness, ruby and sapphire both have a hardness of 9.

Silicon carbide, the abrasive used in grinding wheels and sanding cloth, is only slightly over 9 in hardness. Therefore, wheels and cloth made with this abrasive wear rapidly when used on hard stones, and cutting action is slow.

Although silicon carbide can be used, the favorite abrasive for grinding, sanding, and polishing hard gems is diamond grit. Diamond abrasive costs more initially, but lasts for a long time, and according to suppliers, it is less expensive in the long run. Once the tools are thoroughly impregnated with diamond, only a small amount is needed from time to time.

Preforming

To reduce grinding wheel wear, do as much preforming as possible on a trim saw. If available, a faceter's trim saw with a thin blade should be used to reduce material waste (see section on trim sawing.) After you have sawed or ground a base and oriented it, mark the cabochon outline on the bottom of the stone. Then saw close to the outline, cutting away as much excess material as possible. When this is done, place the stone, bottom up, on the saw table and cut notches around the periphery. Do not cut ino the outline. Because of the saw's curvature, the notches will be cut farther into the crown than the bottom of the gem, which is desirable. The material between the notches can be broken off with pliers to produce a prefrom with sloping sides. *Note: this treatment works well with large and medium sized stones. In most cases, small stones are taken directly to the grinding wheel.*

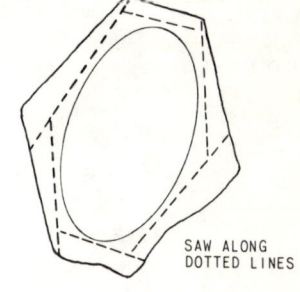

SAW ALONG DOTTED LINES

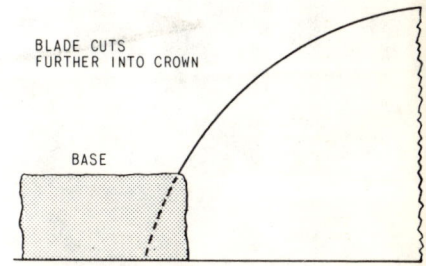

BLADE CUTS FURTHER INTO CROWN

BASE

33 — ADVANCED CABOCHON CUTTING

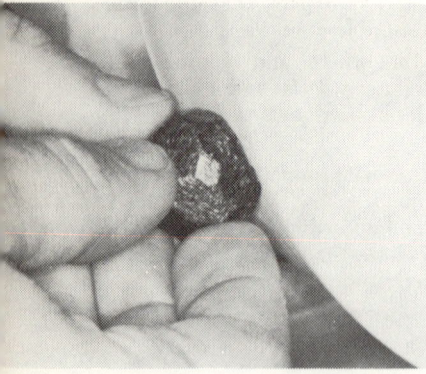

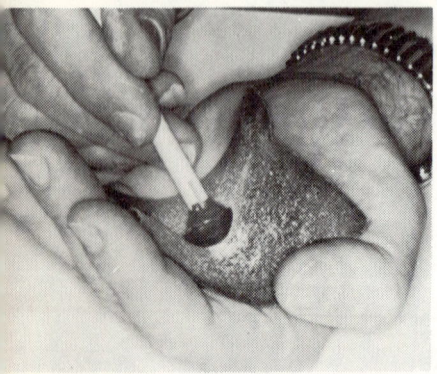

Grinding

For hard gems, a diamond grinding wheel is the fastest and most efficient. This Crystalite Diamond Disc is a metal bonded wheel of medium to coarse grit. Although they are more expensive than silicon carbide, the time saved and the long life of diamond wheels make them well worth it if a large number of gems are to be cut. A diamond wheel should never be used dry. Sweep the stone across the entire wheel surface for even wear. Use moderate pressure. For maximum life a true running arbor is essential. The manufacturer advises a speed of about 700 rpm for this wheel.

Because of the high cost of the diamond wheels, many cutters use silicon carbide wheels. To reduce wear, the wheels should be turned at a fairly high speed (within specified safety limits, of course). Use a light touch and sweep the stone across the face of the wheel. Frequent wheel dressing will probably be required. Although 100 grit wheels are commonly used, some experts advise using only a 220 grit wheel; it is slower, but the fine wheel does not cut deep, hard-to-remove scratches.

Note: a common characteristic of ruby and sapphire is a marked variance in hardness. To avoid grinding away too much material in soft spots, rotate the stone continuously as you grind and smooth it.

Smoothing

A simple way to remove the flat spots left by the grinding wheel is to first sand the gem by hand. Cup a small piece of 120 dry silicon carbide cloth in the hand and rock and rotate the stone against the cloth. In a short time the flat spots will disappear.

Although it is a slow process, smoothing can be done on silicon carbide sanding cloth. The grit will break down rapidly, so use new cloth. Sand on 220, then 400 and 600 grit cloth, either wet or dry. Be sure to wash your hands, the stone, and dop stick between grits.

Rubber Bonded Wheels

Rubber wheels impregnated with silicon carbide, such as the Cratex and

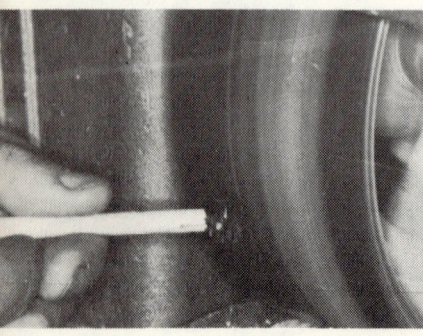

ADVANCED CABOCHON CUTTING — 34

Bright Boy wheels, work well for smoothing hard stones. The wheels do not wear away as fast nor does the grit break down as rapidly as sanding cloth. However, the wheels have little resiliency, and the gem must be turned continuously to prevent flat spots. Usually a coarse and a fine wheel are used. All smoothing on the coarse wheel is done wet. The first smoothing on the fine wheel is also done wet. The gem can then be burnished by smoothing it on the fine grit wheel running dry. This develops considerable heat; check the stone frequently and cool it to prevent cracking and melting the dop wax. If there are any cracks in the stone, you should not run it dry on the rubber bonded wheel because the cracked areas will undercut, enlarging the cracks.

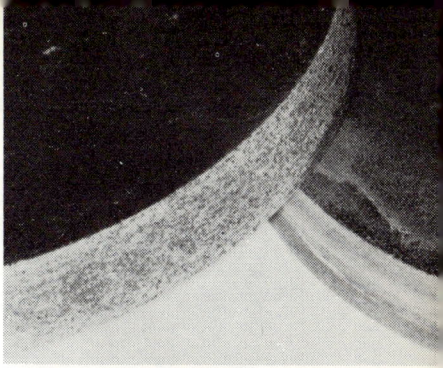

Smoothing With Diamond

Diamond grit and diamond compounds are very popular today and are used on a variety of tools for both smoothing and polishing. Grit sizes available range from 325 to 100,000.

Diamond powder must be mixed with a carrying agent. Some cutters mix it with kerosene or light oil in a small jar. Soon the grit sinks to the bottom. To apply the abrasive to a tool, dip to the bottom with your finger or a piece of hard leather. Kerosene or oil is added as a lubricant from time to time by dipping into the top of the jar. The grit may also be mixed in a small container with lipstick which is an excellent carrying agent.

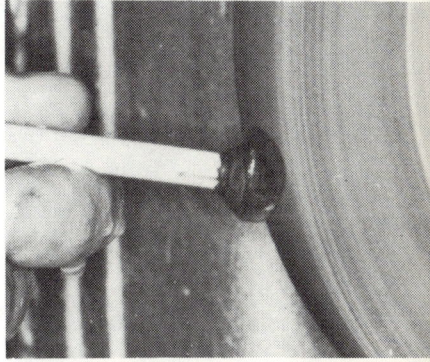

Diamond compounds are very convenient to use. They come in handy applicator syringes so that they may be applied directly to the tool. The carrying agent is water soluble which facilitates cleaning.

Many types of equipment are used for smoothing and polishing with diamond abrasive and compound, and new designs are introduced continually. Because of the fast cutting and cleanliness, this method becomes increasingly popular.

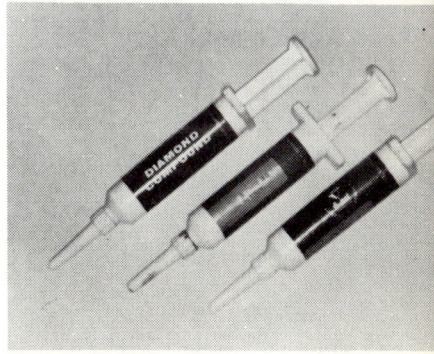

Sapphire Cups

These cups from M.D.R. Manufacturing Co. are made specifically for smoothing and polishing hard stones. The aluminum holder is screwed onto the spindle of a faceting machine or any half-inch vertical arbor. Then a copper cup is inserted into the holder and the retaining ring screwed on to hold it in place. A different cup should be used for each grit.

Smear some 600 diamond compound or diamond grit mix in a cup and start the machine. If possible, run the machine at about 600 rpm until the cup is charged. To charge, rub the cabochon in the revolving cup. This will press the diamond particles into the copper. When the diamond has impregnated the copper, the manufacturer advises increasing the speed to 1100 rpm. Another expert cutter runs his sapphire cups at 1750 rpm. On the first few cabochons, it is necessary to add diamond several times. In a short time the cups become well charged, and new diamond is added only occasionally as needed. Because diamond does not break down rapidly, a small quantity yields a great amount of cutting.

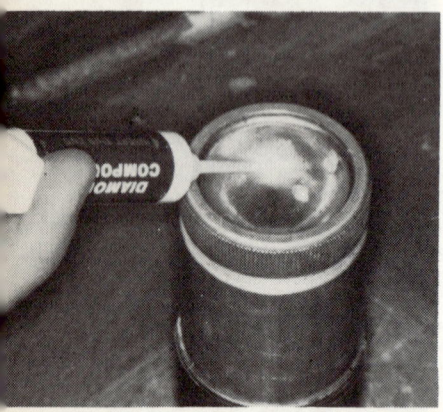

Turn the stone around and around and sweep it from one side of the cup to the other. In time material ground off the stone will form a sludge which impedes cutting action. Flush out the sludge by adding some olive oil, kerosene, or mineral oil. When the marks from previous abrasion have been removed, remove the cup from the holder, and wash the holder, the stone, the machine, and your hands thoroughly. Insert a new cup and charge it with 1200 grit. Smooth the stone and remove the 600 grit marks. Again, clean everything, charge another cup with either 6400 or 8000 grit and work the cabochon again. When you have finished with the 6400 or 8000 grit, the stone should have a fine polish. Be sure to keep the cups separated to avoid contamination.

ADVANCED CABOCHON CUTTING — 36

Grooved hardwood wheels are used on a variety of machines. The grooves may be in the rims of the wheels for running vertically or in the sides for either horizontal or vertical setups. Another innovation is a grooved phenolic fiber lap (second picture from top). Small wooden spools are available (Rohde's Lapidary) that can be used on electric hand drills held in bench mounts. Usually the equipment has some type of speed control.

Absolute cleanliness is a must. Wheels for different sizes of grits must be stored separately in tight containers. The hands, stone and dop stick must be scrupulously clean. On wheels with two grooves in the side, charge the inside groove with fine grit, the outside with coarse so that centrifugal force won't throw the coarse into the fine.

To charge a wheel, first moisten the groove with diamond extender fluid (available from suppliers of diamond compound). Spread the fluid with the cabochon you intend to cut while turning the wheel slowly. Put about a 1/8-inch dab of compound on the cabochon and spread it into the groove while rotating the wheel. When the compound disappears from the stone, apply another dot. You will have to repeat this several times on the first stone, less on the second and finally you will be able to cut several gems without recharging. If you are using loose diamond grit mixed with a carrier, you will probably want to use the carrier as an extender fluid.

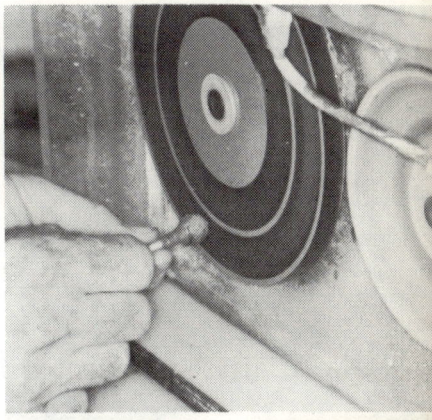

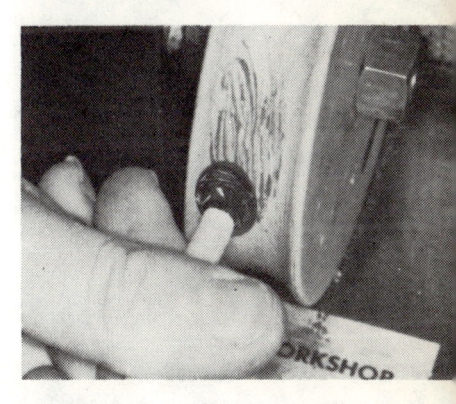

At least two grits are required, 1,200 and 8,000. You will get a better polish if you use 600, 1,200, 3,000 and 8,000, and still better if you finish with 14,000. This sequence will both smooth and polish.

Run the wheels at slow speeds to start, increasing the speed as the diamond impregnates the wheels and the stone begins to smooth. Quite a bit of heat is generated; try to work several stones so that you can alternate. Rock the gems back and forth so that all surfaces are finished. As cutting action slows, add a drop of diamond extender fluid if you're using compound or a drop of light oil for a grit mix. Don't add too much lubricant because it will act as a cushion that keeps the stone from the abrasive.

37 — ADVANCED CABOCHON CUTTING

A newly charged wheel releases abrasive which clings to the stone. With your fingertip (be sure it is clean), smear the grit or compound back on the wheel.

Work each stone on the 600 grit until all scratches are completely gone. If you are using one wheel for each grit, remove the wheel and put it in its individual container. Wash your hands and the stone thoroughly, and repeat the process with the next grit, etc.

Different manufacturers recommend various speeds for their wheels; follow their instructions. Just be sure that you don't run them so fast that they sling off abrasive. You will find that it really doesn't require too much grit or compound to charge the wheels.

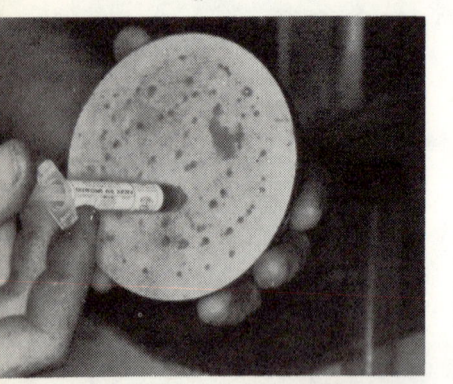

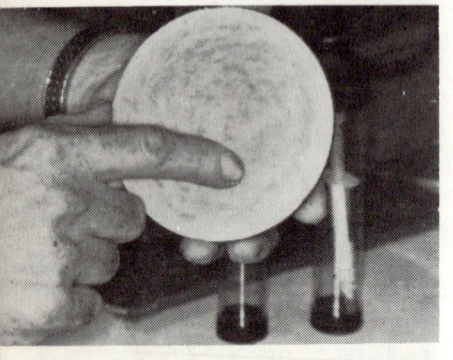

The manufacturer of the phenolic wheels (*Starlaps*), Pacific Test Specialties, recommends the following system: grind on diamond wheels — 260 grit, rough and 1,500 grit, finish; then on starlaps — 1,200 grit, prepolish and 8,000 grit, polish.

The same firm supplies *Crystalpads*, resin treated discs that can be used with diamond compound to smooth and polish hard stones. They must be attached to firm rubber discs which the company also produces. After grinding (see above), the manufacturer advises smoothing away the rough spots with a 600 grit diamond impregnated file (available from rock shops). Recommended grits for use with the pads are: 600, prepolish; 3,000, polish; 8,000, super polish.

To charge a crystalpad apply tiny dots of diamond compound (see picture), using about 2/10 gram for the charge. With your fingertip, spread the compound evenly across the pad. Next add a few drops of diamond extender fluid and finish spreading the abrasive with your finger.

Recommended speed is between 300 and 600 rpm. Rotate the stone as you work it and check frequently. The gem can be kept cool by adding a drop of extender fluid to it or the pad. Because quite a bit of heat is generated with hard stones, the manufacturer advises dopping with epoxy (see page 40).

Another medium that has been used with diamond grit and compound is the hard leather buff. Also, there are Imperial Cabbing Discs and Strips from 3M Company (available at rock shops).

ADVANCED CABOCHON CUTTING — 38

A Sapphire Sphere

To positively locate and orient the stars in a stone, you can cut it into a sphere (see previous section). To make a sphere of hard gem material, preform it on a coarse grinding wheel as you would any sphere (see *Specialized Gem Cutting*). Miniature sphere makers are available from rock hobby suppliers and they are ideal for this purpose. Here. coarse 60-90 silicon carbide grit its used to cut a sphere of star sapphire. The grit breaks down rapidly and must be replenished often. After the sphere is formed with the coarse grit. wash it thoroughly and dop it. Then smooth and polish half the surface with one of the methods described above. Move the stone constantly to keep its spherical shape. When half the surface is polished. remove the sphere from the dop stick and re-dop to polish the other half. You can saw it in half (see previous section) for a set of matched star stones or keep it as a novelty. Because considerable material is cut away. this method is not advised for expensive stones.

Grinding Round Stones

If you want to cut small to medium round cabochons with domed tops, there are several makes of diamond abrasive cabochon cutters. These may be run in bench-mounted electric hand drills, and other equipment with chucks to hold the cutters. Chunks of gemstone are attached to short dop sticks, dipped in water and pushed into the revolving cutters. They are ground for a few minutes, dipped in water again, worked in the cutter, etc., until shaped.

The round cabochon can be smoothed and polished by the methods described above, or you can use a piece of flared copper tubing. The end of the tubing is formed on a flaring tool which you can purchase at a hardware store (inexpensive flaring tools are sometimes found on hardware bargain counters). Clamp the tube in a chuck on a motor shaft or electric drill on a stand. Put some diamond compound on the cabochon and work it in the tube.

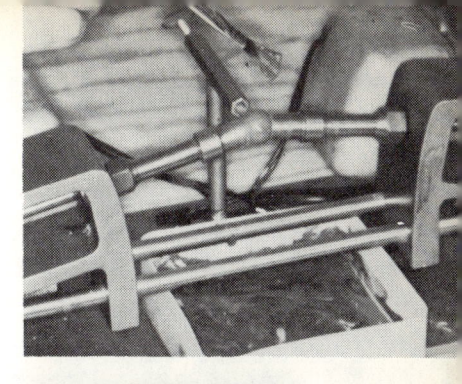

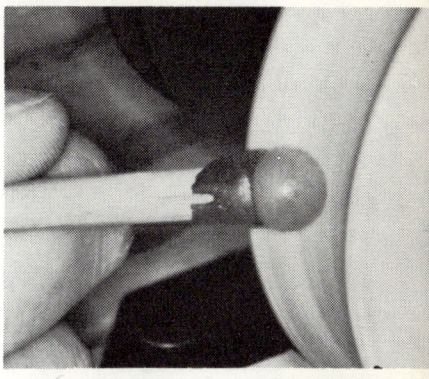

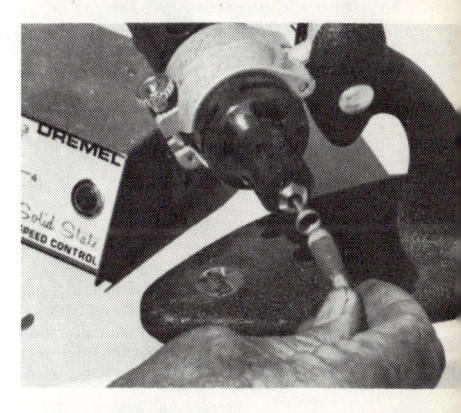

39 — ADVANCED CABOCHON CUTTING

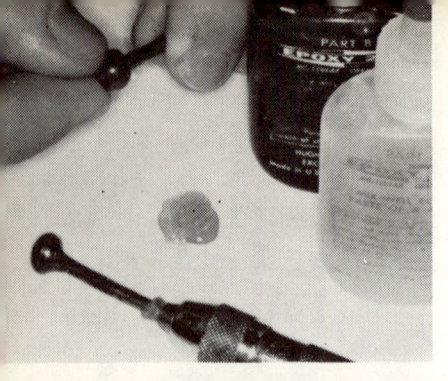

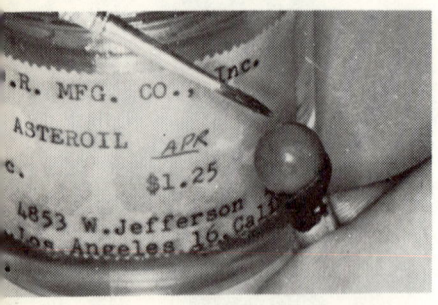

Dopping

Dop a cabochon of hard material at the same cutting stage that you would any other gem. Many rubies, sapphires, and chrysoberyls are small. It is often advisable to dop them at the beginning. See the dopping section for hints on dopping small stones. Because high cutting temperatures are generated, hard stones are often dopped with epoxy. You can remove the stone with a fine saw or Sherwin Williams Wash-Away Paint Remover.

Helpful Hints

As you cut, check the stone frequently for the star or cat's-eye. Oil it and hold it under a strong light. One of the immersion fluids available from rock hobby suppliers is excellent for this purpose. Usually, after using 600 grit diamond, the phenomenon will become evident. If the star or eye is off center, reorient the base.

Remember that the hardness varies in ruby and sapphire. Never let the stone remain in one position while grinding and smoothing, or you may develop a soft spot. Some cutters prefer to start cutting at the girdle, turning the stone round and round gradually increasing the angle — a method referred to as "peeling the apple." However, one expert warns that because of the lamellar partings in Australian black star sapphire and some rubies, the stone should be worked from the crown to the girdle. Each cutter should work out the best procedure for his personal touch. Be sure to practice on some inexpensive stones before cutting a really good one. Ruby and sapphire are available for a few cents a carat to stones costing thousands of dollars.

The favorite diamond grit sizes seem to be 600, 1200, and 6400. Some experienced cutters are able to smooth the stones well enough to go directly to 1200 diamond. Other experts prefer 8000 instead of 6400, and some use both. Some lapidaries use 3000 grit between the 1200 and 6400 or 8000. The 14000 grit is extremely fine and used for a superb final finish. What grits you use depends on your personal touch and how much you care to invest in diamond abrasive. Beginners are safe in starting with the three popular sizes.

Although a slow process, hard stones may be polished on hard buffs with tripoli or Linde A powder. Probably the polish will not be as good as that from diamond. Oldtime lapidaries polished sapphires with tripoli on hard felt

Sources of Equipment and Supplies
For Cutting Hard Stones

The equipment and supplies discussed in this chapter may be purchased at rock shops and from mail-order suppliers. In the past few years, diamond grinding wheels, grit and compound have become increasingly popular. At one time wheels were quite expensive, but now, with new technology, they are offered at prices that hobbyists can afford. The introduction of synthetic diamond has also had a beneficial effect.

Manufacturers are continually introducing new machinery for use with diamond abrasives. Most of them advertise in rock hobby magazines, such as GEMS and MINERALS, P.O. Box 687, Mentone, California 92359. Many of the manufacturers put out literature which is available at rock shops or by writing the advertisers.

ADVANCED CABOCHON CUTTING — 40

Gems & Minerals

GEM CUTTER'S HANDBOOK

CUTTING OPAL

To many gem enthusiasts, opal is the queen of gems. A piece of precious opal with its scintillating flashes of fiery color is indeed a breathtaking sight.

In addition to the precious material, there is common opal. This material is usually opaque and may be white or colored. Some of it contains tree-like patterns known as dendrites. The popular opalized wood from Washington and other sources is also common opal. Pastel shades of common opal and opalized wood are cut into attractive stones.

Precious opal comes from four main sources, Australia, Mexico, Honduras, and the United States. Today, Australia and Mexico are the main sources.

Except for one exception, precious opals exhibit the phenomenon called *play of color*. Radiating from within the stone are flashes of color known as *fire*. The play of color is caused by reflections from a natural defraction grating within the stone. These gratings are made up of submicroscopic silica spheres oriented into a three dimensional lattice. (A complete discussion of the play of color in opal will be found in GEMS & MINERALS, June 1965.)

The only precious opals that do not always exhibit play of color are translucent to transparent gems, either colorless or with body colors of red, yellow, orange or brown. The clear colorless stones are called water opals; the colored ones are known as *fire opals*. Either type may or may not have play of color. Water and fire opals are popular faceting materials. *Note: Many cutters refer to any opal exhibiting play of color (fire) as fire opal. This is incorrect.*

Other opals that exhibit play of color are:
1. White opal — semitranslucent gems with a white or light gray body color. These gems are probably the most common. The more translucent stones exhibit a better play of color.
2. Black opal — stones with dark gray, black, deep blue, green, brown or other dark body colors. These gems are the most highly prized and are usually quite expensive.
3. Jelly opal — translucent to transparent gems, usually with gray, blue, or green body colors. These opals are often used for doublets because they are so clear that the play of color does not show up unless the stones are backed. Occasionally, jelly opals with denser body colors are found that do not require backing; these stones are held in high esteem by gem enthusiasts.

Opals are also classified by the patterns of the play of color. Harlequin opals have small even patches of color. Pinfire opals exhibit tiny dots or patches of color. The colors in flame opal seem to flow across the stone like licking flames. Flash opals exhibit a solid sheet of color.

Note: The Handbook is concerned with gem cutting techniques. Complete information on opals, their sources, varieties, color patterns, etc., can be found in THE OPAL BOOK by Frank Leechman.

41 — ADVANCED CABOCHON CUTTING

CUTTING OPAL

Opal is soft about 5½ to 6½ in hardness. It is a fragile, heat sensitive stone that should be treated gently. Contrary to popular belief, it is not a difficult gem to cut. The most difficult procedure is orienting the stones for best play of color. This requires practice. It is a good idea to purchase a low-cost packet of practice opal before tackling expensive material. One expert advises beginners to cut some obsidian first, because it is similar in hardness and cutting characteristics to opal. If you follow the cutting techniques outlined in this section you should have no trouble.

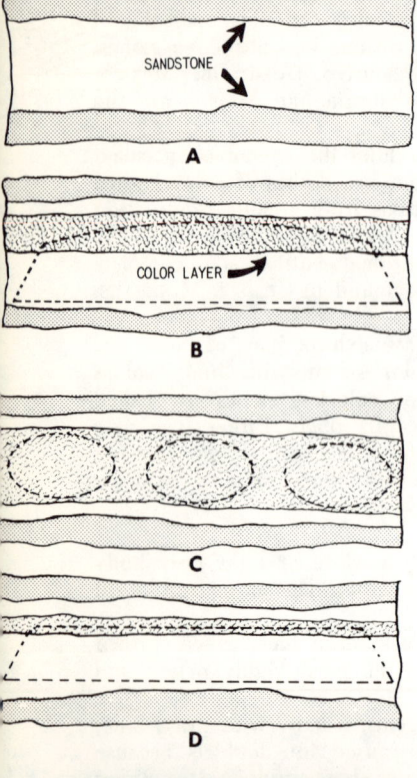

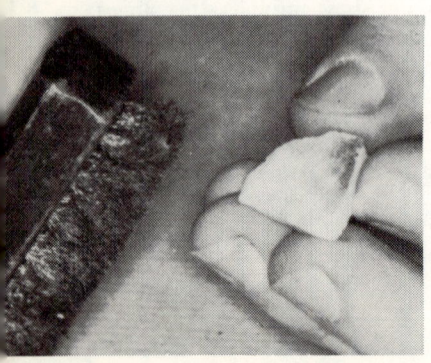

Orienting Australian Opal

Much Australian opal is found in thin seams in a sandstone overburden. When it is chipped out of the mother rock, some of the sandstone usually adheres.

Opals from this type of deposit (Fig. A) are usually tabular with sandstone on the top and bottom. The play of color is visible from the edge. Sometimes the fire (play of color) is distributed evenly throughout the stone. Such a gem is desirable because orientation is not much of a problem. Often the fire is in layers. If the layers are thick (Fig. B) orientation is relatively simple. The stone can be cut so that the fire extends across the crown. Sometimes thick opals are found with wide bands of fire. These can be cut with the base parallel to the edge (Fig. C). Such stones are desirable because the fire is usually more intense. Frequently, the layers of color are thin (Fig. D). In this case, orientation and cutting are more difficult. It is necessary to orient the stone with a color band at the top, and grind and smooth carefully so that you do not cut through the color band.

Before orienting an opal, try to brush away as much sandstone and dirt as possible with a wire brush. Besides sandstone, some opals have thin coatings of iron oxide. This can be removed with sanding cloth or by soaking the stones in a cool solution of oxalic acid. *Warning: oxalic acid is poisonous; handle with care.*

ADVANCED CABOCHON CUTTING — 42

Place the opal in a dish of lukewarm water under a bright light. Turn the stone and examine it to determine where the most intense fire is located. Check to see if the layers of fire extend completely through the stone.

The color layers in seam opal may run parallel to the top and bottom of the stone (Fig. E), or they may be tilted (Fig. F). Where the layers are tilted, the stone must be ground or sawed so that the base is parallel to the layers. If there are several fire layers (Fig. G), it may be possible to saw the stone into pieces so that each layer may be used. This may make the pieces so thin that they must be cemented to a backing material, making them doublets. On high quality opal with good fire, this is desirable. If there is only one band of fire, plan to cut the stone so that the fire is at the top. Try to determine which will be the top and which will be the bottom of the gem.

Sometimes pieces of sandstone are found with a thin seam of opal running through the center. As you inspect such a piece, check to see if there is enough fire and if the opal is thick enough to saw the opal layer in half (Fig. H). If so, the stone can be sawed, so that you will have two opal cabochons. This type is cut so that the sandstone forms the back of the finished gem (Fig. I). If the seam is thin or the fire only in one band, one portion of the sandstone is removed and a single cabochon cut (Fig. J).

When you have studied the fire and the cutting possibilities, hold the opal before a bright light. Unless the stone is very large or very opaque, the light will shine through it, and you should be able to observe flaws and inclusions. Sometimes some of the sandstone matrix extends down through the opal. These spots are waste areas. Try to determine how large a stone you will be able to cut without inclusions.

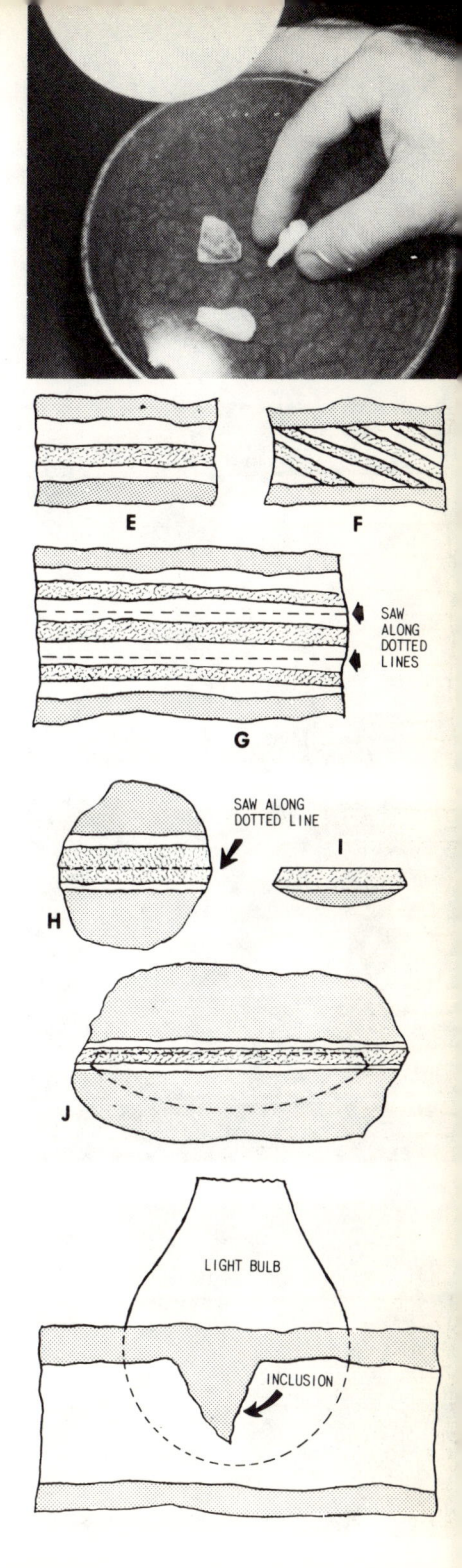

— ADVANCED CABOCHON CUTTING

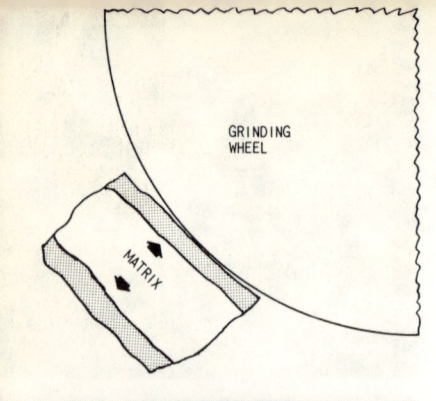

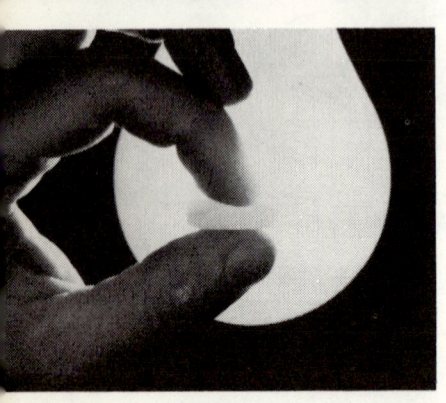

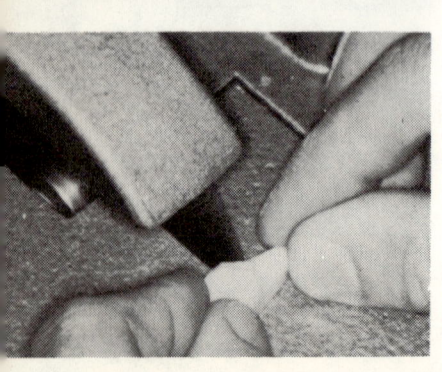

When you have observed the opal thoroughly and have an idea how you will cut it, the matrix should be cut away. This is usually done on a grinding wheel. If there is a fair amount of matrix, you can first use a coarse, 100 or 180 grit wheel. Be sure that the wheel is dressed, free of bumps and smooth. A bumpy grinding wheel can fracture an opal. Use very light pressure and plenty of water. When you have ground away most of the matrix or when there is only a thin coating, use the fine, 220 grit grinding wheel. Remove the matrix and any coatings from the top, bottom, and edges of the opal. You can also remove the matrix and coatings with a flat lap plate and medium grit; 220 grit works well. Other tools that are convenient for removing matrix are 3M Diamond Lapping Discs and Crystallite Diamond Preforming Discs (See section on cutting hard stones). As you begin to grind into the opal, check frequently to make sure you do not grind through a layer of fire. If at all possible, hold the stone by hand. However, it may be necessary to dop small stones, especially if you are lapping them. For lapping, it's handy to dop the stone to a wood block. Lapping grit obscures the stone; be sure to wipe it off frequently and check to make sure you are not lapping through a layer of fire. When the matrix has been ground away, check the stone again to locate the best fire. At this point you should be able to decide which side will be the crown. Next, hold the gem before a light and look for inclusions and flaws. One large cabochon is more valuable than two small ones. However, two small perfect stones are worth more than a large, flawed one.

Small opals are usually taken directly to the grinding wheel. Larger ones from which several gems can be cut or stones in which several layers of fire are to be utilized are sawed. A faceter's trim saw with a thin blade should be used to conserve gem material. A few faceters' saws have vises which will hold small

ADVANCED CABOCHON CUTTING — 44

stones. On most saws the stone is held by hand. If the opal is quite irregular in shape, grind a small flat spot on the edge that will rest on the trim saw table. You can also dop the gem to a block of wood. Saw in straight lines using *very little* pressure. As you near the end of the cut decrease the pressure to a bare minimum. Because opal is porous, it can absorb sawing coolant. Consequently, many cutters use only water or a light soluble oil to cool the blade.

Dopping Opals

Australian and other opals are heat sensitive. If they are heated evenly, there is little danger, but uneven heating can fracture them. To avoid uneven heating, use a controlled heating unit such as Gemstone Shop's Safe Dop. You can also warm the stones under a heat lamp or place them in a pan of lukewarm water and bring the water to a boil. For data on these techniques see the dopping section in *Cabochon Gem Cutting*.

For maximum safety, opals can be cold dopped. Lapidabrade's Stik-Tite cold dop cement is made just for this purpose. Epoxy, sodium silicate, and Duco household cement are other cold dopping favorites. To make a support for the stone, sodium silicate or Duco cement can be mixed with corn starch. Coat the bottom of the stone and the end of the dop stick with adhesive, then press the adhesive and cornstarch dough on the stick and stone. Unite the stone and stick, and shape the dough to support the stone. Let it set until thoroughly dry. With epoxy, use a large diameter dop stick to support the stone.

To remove a stone dopped with wax, place it in a glass of ice water for a short while. The wax will become brittle and the stone will snap off. *Do not try to remove an opal by placing it in a freezer. Opals contain water, and freezing will fracture them.* To remove a stone dopped with epoxy, soak it in Sherwin-Williams Wash-Away Paint Remover or cut it off with a fine-tooth saw. Duco cement is soluble in acetone, sodium silicate in warm water.

45 — ADVANCED CABOCHON CUTTING

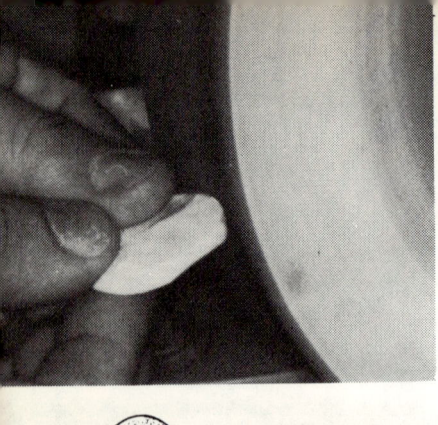

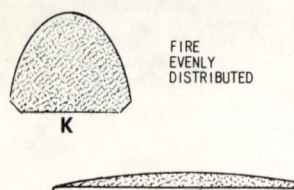

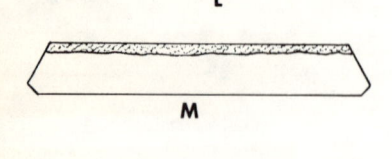

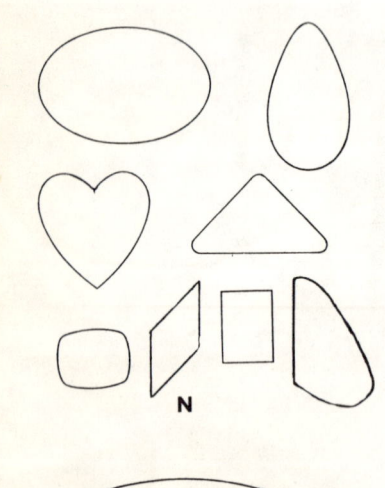

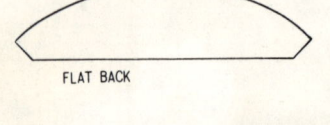

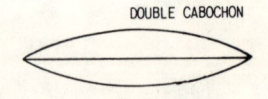

Grinding Opals

It cannot be emphasized too much that opals must be ground on a smooth wheel. Beginners will find it advisable to use only the 220 grit wheel. After some experience, a 100 grit wheel may be used where quite a bit of material is to be removed. After much practice, some cutters use only a 100 grit wheel, but they must be careful not to grind away too much material. Use plenty of water and a *light* touch. Even though it is running wet, a fine grit wheel can sometimes overheat a stone. Check frequently to make sure the opal is not getting too hot. *Note: experienced cutters often run grinding wheels at regular or fast speed. Beginners are advised to reduce the speed.*

K — FIRE EVENLY DISTRIBUTED

L — FIRE

M

If fire is distributed evenly throughout the stone you can grind a high crowned cabochon (Fig. K) if you wish. There is no set rule as to how high the crown must be although most opals are ground with medium to low crowns. Stones with thin layers of fire must be ground as low buff topped cabochons (Fig. L). If the fire layer is very thin, it may be necessary to make the top flat (Fig. M). This is commonly done with seam opals. The most important thing to remember in grinding precious opals is to conserve material. If your stone has excellent fire, do not grind away any more material than you have to. You can cut ovals, rectangles, free forms, etc. (Fig. N). Follow the fire and the natural shape of the stone to make the stone as large as possible. It is much more economical to have a mounting made to fit a fine gem than to grind it away to fit a standard setting. If you are cutting low cost material with no unusual fire, it is best to grind it to a standard size. Opals may be cut with flat bases or as double cabochons. Gem enthusiasts commonly cut them as double cabochons with the front and back polished.

N

FLAT BACK

DOUBLE CABOCHON

ADVANCED CABOCHON CUTTING — 46

Smoothing

For very fine grinding and smoothing, rubber bonded wheels such as Cratex and Brite Boy may be used. One cutter grinds fine opals on a coarse grit Cratex wheel. If an opal has been ground on a ceramic bonded silicon carbide wheel or a diamond wheel, it can be smoothed with a fine rubber bonded wheel using plenty of water. Because of heat, it is not advisable to use the rubber bonded wheel dry. After using the rubber bonded wheel it may be desirable to finish smoothing with abrasive cloth.

The majority of gem cutters probably use silicon carbide abrasive cloth to smooth opals. Well worn wet cloth with plenty of water is advised for beginners. Although it takes longer, using only a well worn 400 and 600 grit will prevent deep scratches. Many cutters use 220 grit first with good results. Use a light touch on all grits, rocking and rotating the gem to avoid flat spots. If you have smoothed the opal on a rubber bonded wheel try finishing with a *well* worn 600 grit cloth. If you use a dry sander, check for heat frequently. It is best to smooth several stones on a dry sander, working each for a short time only.

An old smoothing method employed by a few cutters is silicon carbide grit on wood. A lap of end-grain wood works best. The lap should be grooved to accommodate the shape of the stone. Two laps are needed, one for medium (320) and one for fine grit (400 or 600). Mix the grit with water, and brush it into the wood. Then start the motor. An 8-inch lap should run about 225 rpm. Rock the stone back and forth to avoid flat spots. When it is well smoothed on the medium grit, wash everything and repeat with fine. A fine matte finish results which should buff into a glossy polish.

Because they give cool, smooth, fast cutting, diamond grinding wheels and the various smoothing and polishing accessories for use with diamond abrasive are now very popular. These tools and methods are covered in the fifth chapter of this book and in *Specialized Gem Cutting*.

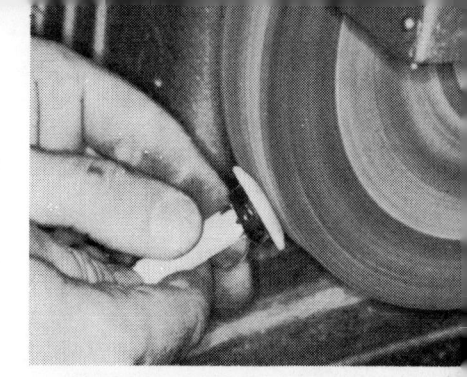

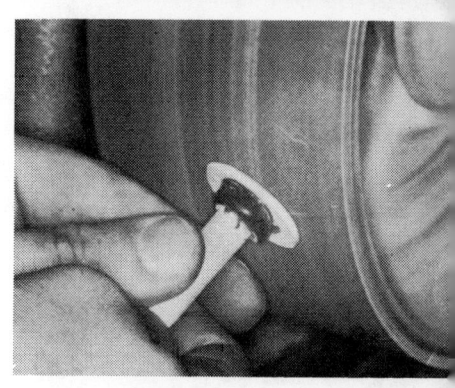

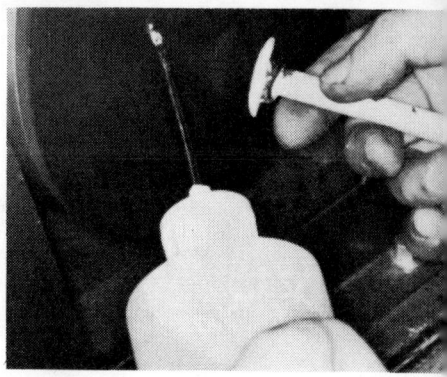

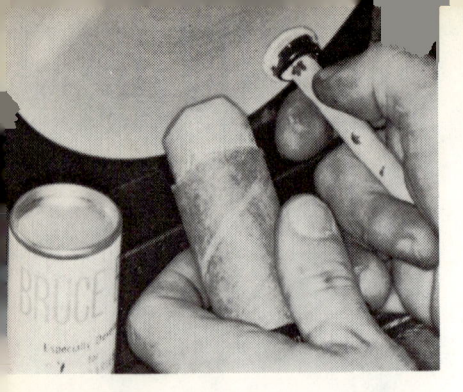

Prepolishing is used by some experts to put a final gloss on the stone before polishing. Use a leather (rough side out), felt, canvas, or Pellon buff for prepolishing. Mix some fine grit (1,000 or finer) silicon carbide and water, and brush the mixture into the buff while it is not in motion. Start the motor (run at motor speed or slower) and rock and rotate the stone against the buff. Add some water from the grit mixture frequently, and some more grit occasionally. A handy 1,000 grit Bruce Bar may be used instead of the water and grit mixture. Add water as you buff the stone. Tripoli may be used in lieu of silicon carbide.

Polishing

The all around favorite for polishing opal seems to be cerium oxide on a felt buff. However, many other combinations are used: Linde A on leather; tin oxide on leather, muslin, felt, velvet, canvas, or Pellon; cerium oxide or rough on any of the common buffs, etc. Rouge on muslin is used by some as a final polish after using one of the other combinations. The polishing combination is not nearly so important as a good preliminary smoothing job. If the stone is not well smoothed, you cannot get a good polish. As mentioned on the previous page, diamond abrasive is becoming increasingly popular for both prepolishing and polishing opals. Many cutters now use diamond compound on resin treated pads or wooden wheels. If you use wooden wheels, try to work several stones so that you may rotate them as they become warm. This method produces a beautiful polish.

Whatever polishing combination you use, keep the gem cool. Felt buffs can generate lots of heat in a small area which can crack an opal. Contrary to popular methods, many professionals and experts run their buffs fast and wet. About 1750 rpm for a 6- or 8-inch buff is the speed prescribed by some professionals. *However, you must keep the buff wet.* If you are using a mixture of polishing compound and water, add some of the water from the top of the mixture frequently. If you are using a Bruce Bar, add fresh water with a brush or squeeze bottle.

Be sure that the buff you use for opal is not contaminated with grit. Even a little speck of grit can cause a monstrous scratch. Keep everything scrupulously clean.

The instructions in this section are primarily for Australian opal with play of color. The next section will review additional types of Australian opals, as well as opals from other parts of the world. Hints for using tiny opal chips, making doublets, preserving opals and other important subjects will be covered.

ADVANCED CABOCHON CUTTING — 48

Gems & Minerals

GEM CUTTER'S HANDBOOK

CUTTING OPAL
Part 2 — Special Techniques

The previous section covered the orientation and cutting of Australian opal. The cutting steps explained will suffice for most opal from Australia or other sources. All opal is heat sensitive, and must be dopped, smoothed, and polished carefully. All opal is relatively soft and fragile, and must be handled gently.

A few varieties of opal require special cutting techniques. Both Australia and Mexico produce opal in matrix. The polishing technique for the Australian stones differs from that of the Mexican gems. Special cutting techniques are also required for Australian boulder opal, Nevada's Virgin Valley opal, and some Honduras material. These techniques and other special cutting hints are covered in this section.

Australian Matrix Opal

Matrix opal from Australia is composed of ferriferous sandstone, locally called ironstone, shot through with tiny bits of precious opal. The opals are much too small to cut individually, therefore the entire mass is cut into a cabochon. Grinding and smoothing are relatively simple, but the difference in composition between the opal and matrix can cause polishing difficulties. One expert polishes opal matrix twice. First he uses cerium oxide on felt to polish the opal. Next he polishes the ferriferous matrix on leather with rouge. Other experts polish only on leather with rouge. Occasionally a dark grey matrix is found containing black opal. This material is held in high esteem.

PATCHES OF PRECIOUS OPAL

Some Australian matrix opal has been heat-treated to simulate black opal. When processed properly, these stones are quite beautiful. The first stones of this type were treated only after being cut as a cabochon. The cabochons were first put into heat-controlled ovens, then soaked in a sugar solution, and finally placed in sulphuric acid which carbonizes the sugar, turning the stone black. This process is now used on rough matrix opal and the treated rough is sometimes available to hobbyists. After a cabochon is cut from this rough it may be necessary to treat it once more. Dealers who sell the rough matrix supply instructions for treating the finished gems.

49 — ADVANCED CABOCHON CUTTING

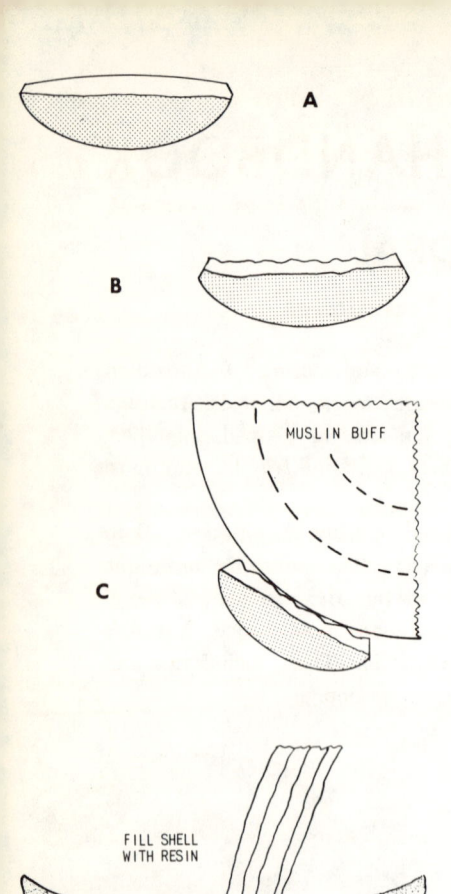

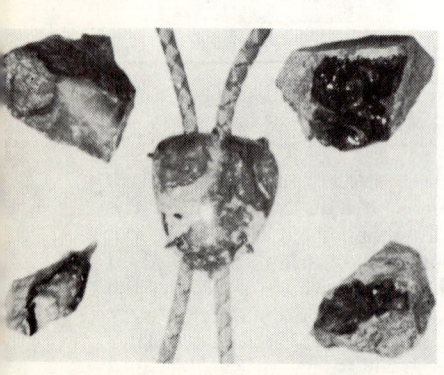

Australian Boulder Opal

Chunks of sandstone are sometimes found in which there are cracks filled with precious opal. The miners usually split these chunks to expose the thin opal layer. Infrequently the layer is thick enough to grind into a low cabochon (Fig. A). Often it is safer to eliminate grinding, and smooth and polish only. Usually, the layer is not thick enough to smooth. In this case, the opal may be left rough and the sandstone cut into a cabochon (Fig. B). Even though it is rough, the opal makes a beautiful gem. Some gem enthusiasts maintain that the broken surfaces are more attractive than polished opal. The beauty of the opal may be enhanced by polishing the rough surfaces with tin or cerium oxide on a muslin buff (Fig. C). Be sure to cut one or two rows of stitching on the buff so that the individual layers will penetrate into the irregularities on the opal's surface (see polishing section).

Opalized Shells

Bone and shells that have been replaced by precious opal are found in some Australian gem fields. Usually these are sold as specimens, but a few are polished and set into jewelry. Most of the shells are too thin to grind, and should be smoothed and polished only. Sometimes it is necessary to strengthen one. The simplest method is to fill it with plastic resin. When the resin has hardened, smooth and polish the shell's exterior.

Mexican Opal

Most Mexican opal is found in a rhyolite matrix. True fire opal is translucent Mexican opal with a red, orange or yellow body color. It may or may not have play of color. Deep red translucent opal is sometimes referred to as cherry opal. Another variety known as water opal is clear or translucent. Mexican opal is cut both as cabochons and faceted stones. The clear and translucent stones with play of color are quite popular with faceting enthusiasts. If the opal area in a matrix stone is large enough to cut by itself, the matrix is ground away, and the opal is oriented and

ADVANCED CABOCHON CUTTING — 50

cut the same as Australian opal. Often the opal areas are small and a cabochon is cut to include the matrix. The rhyolite matrix is about the same in hardness and does not require special polishing; cut the matrix stone as if it were solid opal. Some Mexican opal has checks and cracks in the surface. These cracks may be ground away but usually more develop in the surface of the cut gem. Try to purchase flawless material.

Opal from the United States

Common opal and opalized wood occurs in several of the United States. Precious opal has been found in Texas, New Mexico, Idaho, Washington, Oregon, California and Nevada. Of these, the Virgin Valley area in Nevada produces the most.

Virgin Valley opal is a replacement of ancient wood. Much of it shows the tree's growth rings. It is often clear white or black and brilliant colors radiate from within it. Unfortunately, like some Mexican opal, most of the Virgin Valley material develops checks and craze marks after it has been removed from the ground. Several remedies have been prescribed for this problem including drying the stones under intense sunlight, keeping them in water or glycerine except when worn, and burying them in wet clay for several months. None of these methods has been particularly successful. It has been observed that the crazing usually starts at scratches on the gem's surface. Milky areas also develop at the scratches. One expert tried putting a super polish on some Nevada opals, a polish on which he could not focus a ten-power lens. After a few years only a few stones had crazed. Several other cabochons cut from the same piece of rough opal were given just an average polish. Most of these stones developed cracks and milky areas in a short time.

CRACKS DEVELOP AFTER OPAL IS MINED.

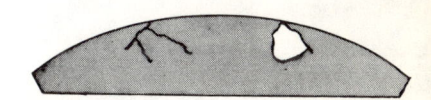

Honduras Opal

Honduras produces several types of precious opal. The white opal from Honduras is quite similar to that from Australia and can be cut in the same way. A thin vein opal can be cut like Australian boulder opal. According to experienced cutters, it is almost impossible to cut Honduras matrix opal because the basalt matrix will not take a polish. One type of Honduras opal requires special treatment. It is found in small nodules resembling geodes. Usually fractures extend from the outside of the nodule into the opal. All fractures must be ground away so that the cabochon is cut from flawless material. If any fractures are not ground away, the finished gem will crack.

CRACKS AND MILKY AREAS DEVELOP IN SURFACE OF FINISHED GEM.

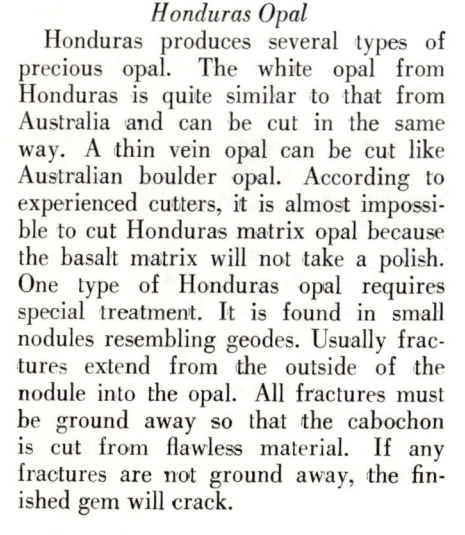

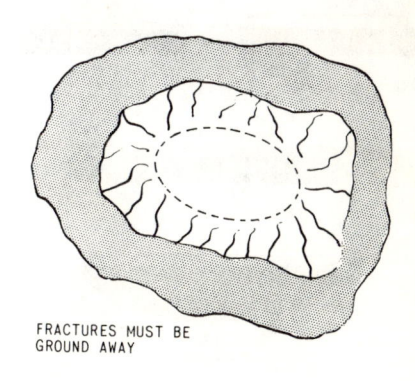

FRACTURES MUST BE GROUND AWAY

Doublets

Frequently pieces of opal with beautiful play of color are encountered that are too thin to cut into cabochons. Also, some opal is of such high quality that it is desirable to section it into thin slices so that several cabochons may be produced. These thin pieces of opal must be cemented to a protective backing before they are cut into finished gems. The assembly is known as a *doublet*. Black, white, and jelly opal are all used for doublets. Backing materials commonly used are common (potch) opal, obsidian, black jade, and black structural glass. Many Australians insist that potch must be used if the doublet is to be called an opal.

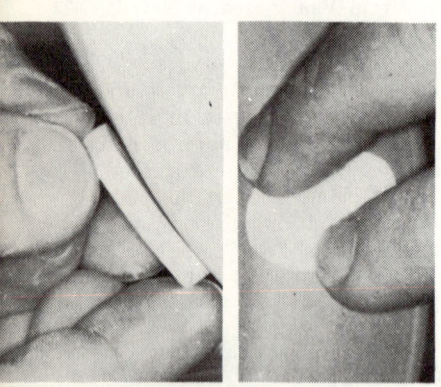

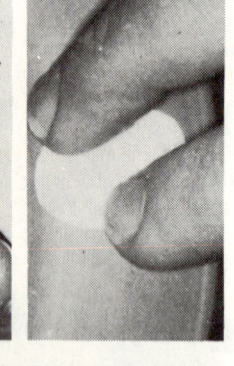

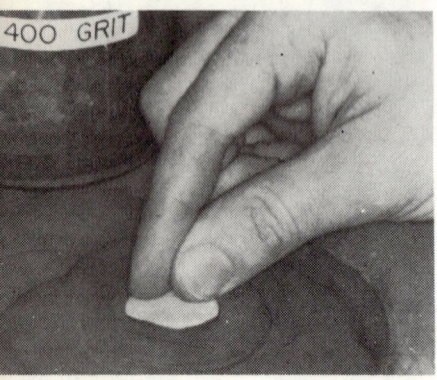

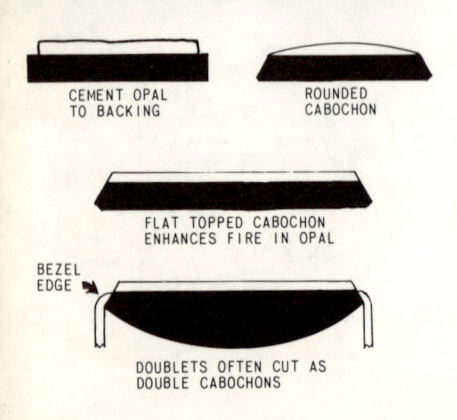

The first step in making a doublet is to remove any matrix from both faces of the opal. If the gem is reasonably thick this can be done on the face or side of a grinding wheel. Use a light touch, and *plenty of water* to avoid cracking the opal. When all matrix and inclusions have been removed, observe the opal from all sides to determine which face should be cemented to the backing and which shows the most attractive fire for the top. The face to be cemented must be flat. This can be done on the side of a grinding wheel, or by hand lapping on plate glass with 220 grit. Finish lapping on glass with 400 grit. Next, put a flat surface on the backing material in the same way. Then cement the two materials together. Many cutters use epoxy. However, some experts advise Canada balsam. Because this adhesive is flexible it allows for any difference in expansion between the two parts of the doublet. If the backing is black, clear cement can be used. If it is not black, add some lampblack or black pigment (available from plastic resin manufacturers) to the adhesive. When the cement has hardened, shape the assembly into a cabochon. Some doublets are finished with rounded tops; many are finished flat or with tops that are only slightly rounded. There are two reasons for the flat tops: (1) some thin seam opal can only be cut this way (2) cutting the opal top until it is very thin intensifies the fire in the stone. Doublets may be cut with flat backs or as double cabochons. A bezel edge should be cut so that the jewelry mounting will crimp onto the backing instead of the thin opal.

CEMENT OPAL TO BACKING

ROUNDED CABOCHON

FLAT TOPPED CABOCHON ENHANCES FIRE IN OPAL

BEZEL EDGE

DOUBLETS OFTEN CUT AS DOUBLE CABOCHONS

ADVANCED CABOCHON CUTTING — 52

Another form of doublet is made by cementing a thin piece of opal to a piece of clear optical quartz. Both the opal and the quartz are lapped on one side for cementing. Use clear cement. When the cement has hardened, cut the assembly so that the quartz forms the top of the doublet. This type of doublet is advised for men's rings because the hard quartz protects the opal. Finished quartz cabochons to make this type of doublet are available from some dealers.

Triplets

An attractive stone can be made by cementing a dark backing to the underside of a quartz-topped doublet. After the doublet is made, lap the opal on the underside until it is paper-thin. Then lap a flat surface on a piece of obsidian or other black material. Cement the black material to the opal. When the cement has hardened, shape the backing so that the doublet will fit a mounting. The black material will intensify the fire in the opal, and the quartz will magnify it. *More tips on making doublets and triplets will be found in the section on assembled stones.*

Jelly Opal

Some jelly opal is translucent and has enough dense play of color that it may be cut and mounted with no backing. Most of this material, however, is transparent or very translucent. To bring out the play of color, this clear jelly opal must be backed with a dark material. It is commonly made into doublets or triplets. A simpler method is to coat the back with black lacquer or epoxy to which black pigment has been added.

Using Opal Chips

Gem cutters sometimes accumulate trimmings from opals they cut. Because of their brilliant play of colors, the chips are too pretty to throw away, but too small to cut. There are several ways in which they may be set into jewelry. One method involves the use of blown glass bulbs. The chips are placed in the bulbs and the bulbs filled with glycerine. Then corks are inserted in the necks of the

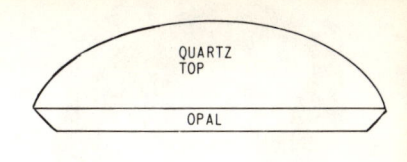

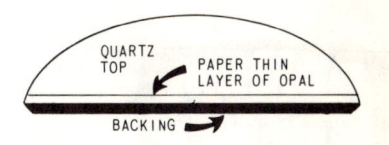

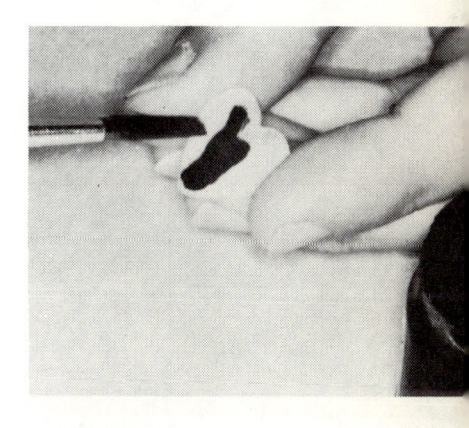

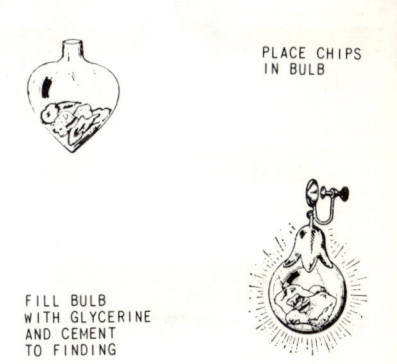

53 — ADVANCED CABOCHON CUTTING

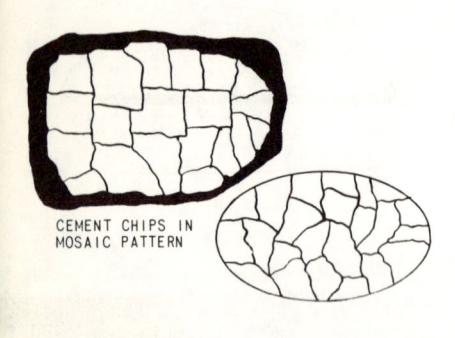

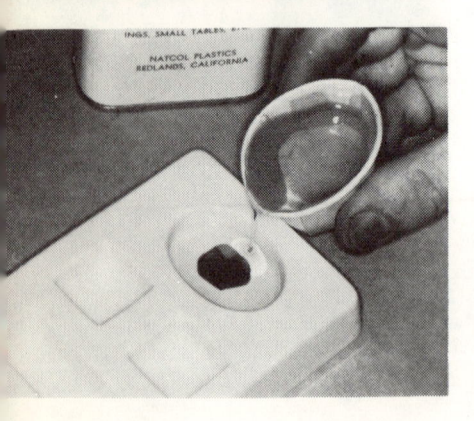

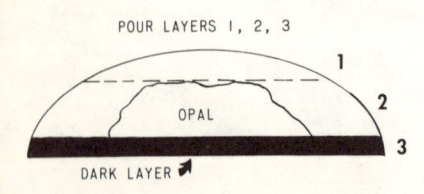

bulbs and the assembly cemented to jewelry findings. The opal floats in the glycerine and its colors flash out.

Small bits of opal may also be cemented to dark cabochons. A piece of white opal on an obsidian cabochon is quite attractive. Finish the cabochon, and then rough the area on which the opal will be cemented with a small piece of 220 or 400 grit abrasive cloth held by hand. Sometimes a bit of rough opal is attractive enough in its natural state to be used without finishing. In other instances, the opal chip looks better if it is first dopped, smoothed and polished. It seldom requires grinding.

A quantity of opal chips can be cemented to a piece of slabbed obsidian. Try to select pieces that will fit closely together. Some careful grinding may be required on the edges of the chips to make them fit. Cement them in place to form an attractive mosaic pattern. When the cement hardens, the assembly can be cut into a cabochon. *Note: remember that grinding the cabochon shape will remove some of the opal's surface. Be sure to place fire layers so that they will not be ground away. If you are using thin chips, make a flat topped cabochon.*

Embedding Opal

To keep Virgin Valley and other types of opal from cracking, it can be embedded in plastic resin. Plastic suppliers have ceramic molds which will produce cabochon shapes of standard size. The resin is mixed and the mold filled to about one-third its depth. When the resin hardens the opal is laid in place and more resin poured in to cover it. Finally, some pigment, usually black, is mixed with catalyzed resin and the last layer poured. This layer forms the back of the "cabochon." This method can also be employed to use opal chips.

Note: Opal chips for mosaics and embedding are sold in bottles or ounce lots by some suppliers.

ADVANCED CABOCHON CUTTING — 54

Cutting Hints

Occasionally when an opal is cut, a cavity or inclusion is encountered that mars the appearance and decreases the value of the stone. The usual solution is to recut the opal into smaller stones. Instead of recutting, you can have a mounting made that will cover the blemish. Jewelry makers can add leaves or other designs that will extend across the surface to hide the imperfection.

DECORATIVE LEAF COVERS BLEMISH

Opals are sometimes found with the fire located in a concave face. Either the stone is too thin to cut into a cabochon, or grinding in reverse to the concave face will cut away the fire layer. Such stones can be carved into leaves, flowers and other shapes which have concave surfaces.

FIRE LAYER

Because opal is soft it can be scratched, especially if it is mounted in a vulnerable spot like a ring. Natural abrasion may cause its surface to become dull. It is possible to repolish an opal without removing it from its setting. Use cerium oxide on a hard leather buff running at *very low speed*. Swipe the mounted opal gently across the surface, checking frequently to make sure it does not overheat. Be careful not to catch any prongs or decorations in the buff. The dull surface will polish quickly. Deep scratches cannot be removed this way, but the improved appearance of the rest of the surface will do much to hide them. When you have finished buffing, remove any cerium oxide with running water and a toothbrush.

A Faceting Tip

Clear Australian and Mexican opal with play of color makes attractive faceted gems. The two types must be treated differently. If the play of color is concentrated in one area in a Mexican opal, this area should be oriented so that it will be near the culet of the finished stone. Conversely, the main play of color in faceted Australian opal should be in the crown.

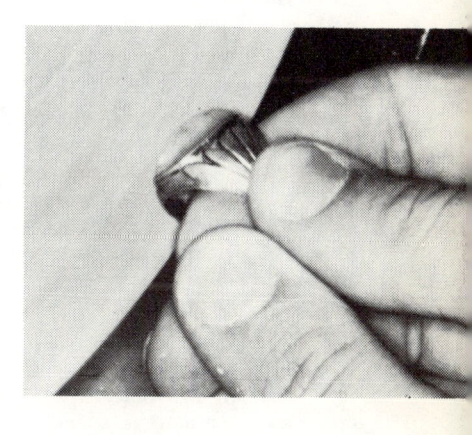

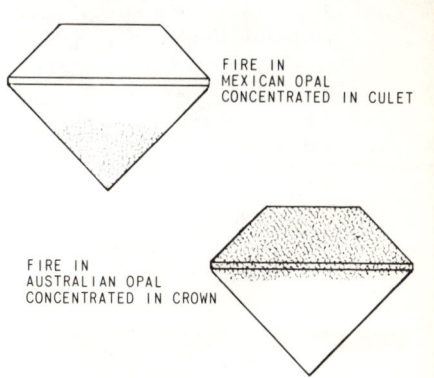

FIRE IN MEXICAN OPAL CONCENTRATED IN CULET

FIRE IN AUSTRALIAN OPAL CONCENTRATED IN CROWN

Helpful Hints

To reduce the amount of heat needed for dopping, first coat the back of the opal with shellac, and let it dry. The shellac will cause the dop wax to stick at a lower temperature. Remember to check for heat at all cutting stages. If you are dry sanding, do not check for heat by holding the stone against the palm of your hand. Oil from your skin will coat it and impede the action of fine sanding cloth. It is much better to sand several stones, smoothing each for a short interval. Be sure to use plenty of water when grinding an opal on the side of a wheel.

Cuttings from stones lodge in sanding cloth. If you have been cutting a harder stone, be sure to clean the cloth before sanding opal. The hard residue can dislodge and scratch the opal. Better yet, use one cloth for opal only. Another method of smoothing opal is to use a mixture of water and fine loose grit on a buff.

Diamond abrasives are also used for making doublets. One hobbyist cuts thin pieces on a trim saw, then grinds almost to the fire layer on a 220 grit wheel. Next he laps on a 260 grit flat diamond disc until the fire is exposed, and finishes up with flat discs in 600 and 1,500 grit, increasing the water flow on the latter. This should bring the stone to a semipolish; if not, it's touched up on a muslin buff with tin oxide. The quartz cap is treated in the same way; then the two stones are *cleaned carefully* with acetone followed by alcohol and cemented with epoxy. Cleanliness is the key; otherwise the cement may not bond. After the cement has hardened, the opal is ground to the right thickness and, if a triplet is being made, the backing stone is lapped flat, cemented on, and thinned if necessary.

It is best to set opal in mountings with thin bezels. If it is to be mounted in a heavy bezel setting, which requires hammering, it should be done by someone with experience so that the stone will not be fractured. In using prong mountings, be sure that the prongs exert even pressure on the opal. Doublets should be set in bezel mountings to conceal the juncture of the assembly. It is not advisable to set an opal in a man's ring that will be worn every day; it will encounter too many knocks and much abrasion. Opals receive less abuse in earrings, pendants, tie tacks, and similar mountings.

Opal contains water. When it is exposed to air, some of the water escapes. When the water content is reduced, some opals crack or craze. It is believed by some experts that these stones have internal stress and that the water acts as a cushion. Consequently, they feel that the escape of the water causes the stones to crack. Various remedies have been tried with little success, including storing the stones in glycerine or water when they are not worn. One expert advises that before an opal is cut, it should be dehydrated to determine if it will crack. He sets his opals in an oven at 100 to 125 degrees or in direct sunlight for a few hours. If they crack, they are not worth cutting.

Do not keep opal jewelry in boxes with other jewelry. Use individual jewelry boxes or keep it in chamois bags. Most of the dust in the atmosphere is 7 in hardness. Dusting an opal with a cloth can rub this dust into the surface. It is best to dust with a feather. Opal is porous, and after it is dehydrated, it will absorb water. Do not immerse it in soapy water; it will absorb the soap which can discolor it.

Gems & Minerals

GEM CUTTER'S HANDBOOK

CUTTING JADE

Gem cutters generally consider polishing jade a challenge. This gem undercuts, and does not respond readily to some of the conventional smoothing and polishing methods. Experts agree that with a little special handling and experimentation it can be polished without difficulty.

The term "jade" actually includes two minerals, nephrite and jadeite. Nephrite is a calcium magnesium silicate with some iron and is an amphibole. In structure it is an aggregate of tiny, interwoven, fibrous crystals. Jadeite is a sodium aluminum silicate and is a pyroxene. It, too, is a crystalline aggregate, but the crystals are granular. Both minerals are extremely tough. They are medium in hardness: nephrite, 6.5 and jadeite, 6.5-7. Both are quite insensitive to heat.

Jade is an excellent carving material; it can be cut quite thin, and delicate pieces can be created without fear of breaking. Cutters not skilled in carving usually cut it into cabochons. The cabochon cutting methods of a number of experts are reviewed in this section. Among these techniques you should find at least one that will enable you to put a lustrous polish on a piece of jade.

Sawing Jade

Large pieces of jade should be reduced by sawing. This material is so tough that attempting to break it with a hammer is not advisable; a rebounding hammer can cause injury. One method of breaking up a jade boulder is to saw a slot in it and pound wedges into the slot. Large chunks are also sawed with grit saws (see section on slab sawing).

The toughness of jade slows down sawing action. To avoid misalignment and blade damage it is advisable to set slab saw carriage feeds on slow speed and to use less pressure in trim sawing. Most cutters find that their regular saw coolant will work for jade. However, one professional cutter who normally uses kerosene as a coolant, switches to a water soluble oil for this material. Another cutter adds one tablespoon of graphite to each gallon of coolant.

Dress the blade after sawing jade.

Because jade does not have the abrasive quality of some materials, it does not wear away the metal bond on diamond saw blades. Consequently blades glaze. Whenever you saw a piece of jade, you should dress the saw blade by cutting through a piece of 220 grit grinding wheel or soft brick. Two cuts through the dressing material will usually "sharpen" the blade satisfactorily.

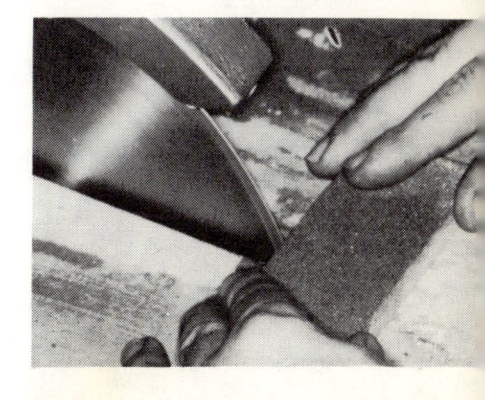

57 — ADVANCED CABOCHON CUTTING

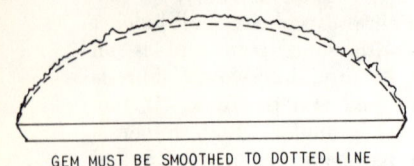

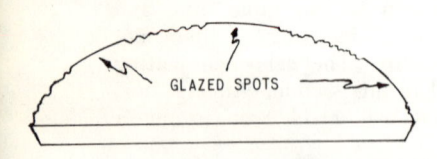

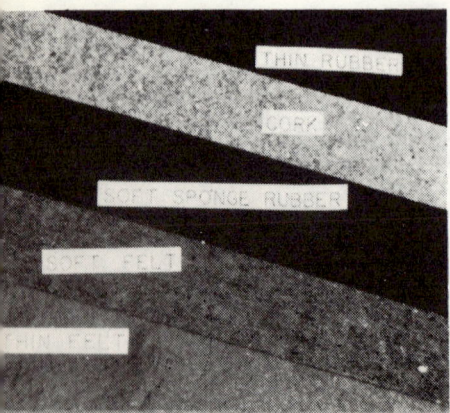

Grinding

There are no particular problems in grinding jade. Most cutters use 100 and 220 grit grinding wheels. A few use 220 and 320 or 400 grit. Others use only a 100 or a 220 grit wheel. The grit is not so important as using a smooth true wheel to avoid undercutting. The wheel should run in plenty of water at all times. It does not take long to grind the medium-hard jade.

Smoothing

When jade is smoothed, the surface must be abraded to the bottom of all the pits and crevices left by grinding (A). At the same time, no new crevices must be created by pulling out some of the interwoven crystals (undercutting). Finally, the gem must be smoothed without prematurely glazing portions of the surface (B). If glazing occurs before the surface is sufficiently abraded, a false polish will appear. When the gem is buffed, it will have a finish resembling an orange peel.

Smoothing With Sanding Cloth

Most cutters use sanding cloth on drums or discs to smooth jade. New cloth with sharp grit is usually employed to abrade the surface without glazing. Some cutters do not break in the cloth. However, this produces deep scratches which may be hard to remove. Most experienced cutters use a new cloth that has just been broken in. (Tip — to break in cloth rapidly, smooth a piece of cheap sapphire or ruby on it.)

Sander Cushions

Most sanding drums and discs are furnished with soft felt or sponge rubber cushions. Jade cutting enthusiasts often replace these cushions with thin rubber or felt. They feel that with a less resilient backing, the abrasive on the sanding cloth cannot bite far enough into the jade to cause undercutting. Some manufacturers produce sanders with slightly resilient cork cushions specifically for jade and other materials which undercut.

Wet or Dry Cloth?

There is no set rule. Experienced cutters use both. The majority now favor wet cloth. Dry cloth must be used carefully because the heat generated in dry sanding can cause premature glazing. There is little chance of glazing with wet cloth running in plenty of water. Several techniques for both dry and wet cloth are described below. It is best to experiment; various types of jade respond to different techniques. If you have a wet sander, try this first.

Wet Sanding

A favorite wet sanding technique is to first smooth the jade with new 220 grit cloth, then with new 400, and finally new 600. Copious amounts of water should be used at all times. If any white spots appear on the gem, more water is needed. Revolve and brush the stone against the cloth with a light, even pressure. When this sanding sequence has been completed, the jade should have a smooth surface with no pits and no glaze. *Note*: some cutters start with 120 or 150 grit wet cloth and continue with 220, 400, and 600. The 120 or 150 grit cloth will cut rapidly; only light pressure should be exerted.

The final step with this technique is to lightly sand the jade on well-worn 600 grit cloth, completely dry. Rock the stone and remove it from the sander frequently to avoid overheating. Soon a gloss will appear, and the gem is ready for polishing.

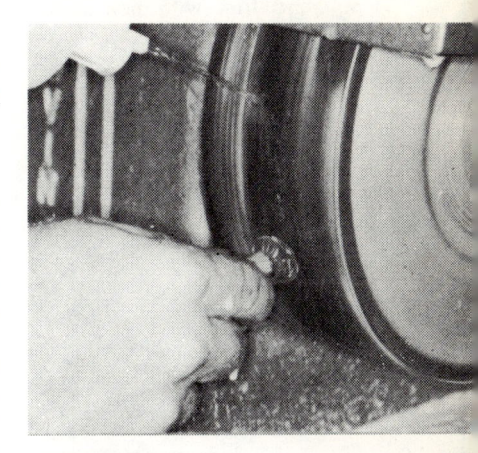

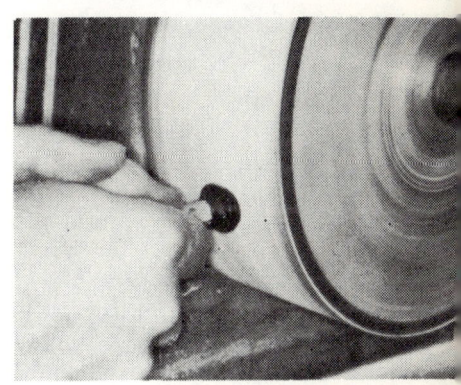

An Alternate Wet Sanding Technique

One experienced professional cutter uses only 400 grit wet cloth for jade. He first grinds the gem on a 100 grit wheel with plenty of water. Then he touches the cabochon lightly on a 220 grit grinding wheel running dry. This finish grinding takes only a few seconds and must be done carefully to avoid overheating and glazing. The jade is then smoothed on new 400 wet cloth that has just been broken in. As the abrasive wears, it will cut a progressively smoother surface. Plenty of water should be applied to the sander.

Dry Sanding

More skill and caution are required to dry-sand jade. It is advisable to sand several stones to avoid overheating and glazing. There are several techniques:

1. Sand first with new 220 grit cloth, then with new 320. Touch the stone lightly to the cloth, and avoid overheating. If done properly, there will be no glaze.
2. First grind the gem on 100, 220, and 400 grit grinding wheels. Then smooth first with new 320 grit cloth and then with well worn 320 cloth. Put a gloss on the jade with the worn cloth.
3. Sand first with new 220 grit cloth and then finish smoothing with well worn 220 grit.

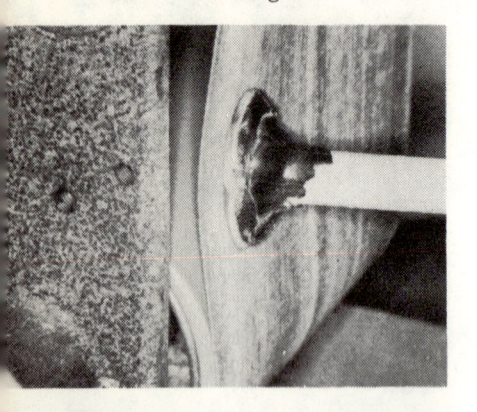

Belt Sanders

Although the majority of experienced cutters prefer sanders with a firm backing, at least one expert has used a belt sander with no backing at all. The jade was ground to a rough contour on a coarse wheel. Final shaping and preliminary smoothing were done with a 120 grit belt. Then 220 and 320 grit belts were used for intermediate and final smoothing. A semi-polish was produced with the 320 cloth.

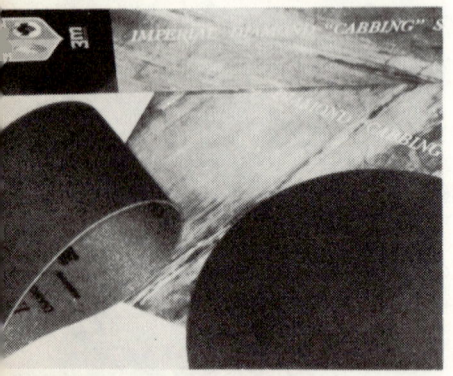

Diamond Abrasives

As noted in previous chapters, diamond abrasives are used more and more for cutting a variety of gemstones. These work to particular advantage with jade, especially in smoothing, prepolishing and polishing, because the diamond stays sharp and cuts rapidly which reduces undercutting. Glazing is prevented because the work stays cool. Follow the manufacturer's instructions and those in foregoing chapters or *Specialized Gem Cutting* for whatever type abrasives you use.

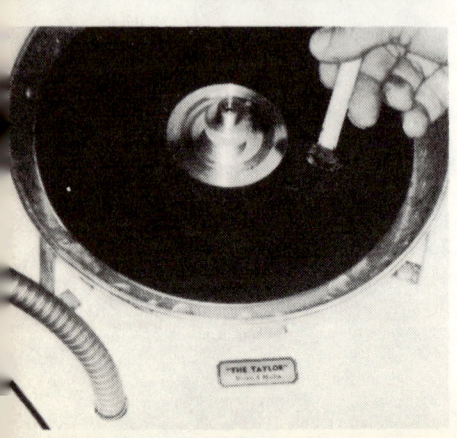

A few cutters use faceting laps to smooth jade. A diamond lap with 1200 grit or its equivalent should be used. The lap should be protected by using only light pressure and not allowing sharp edges to dig into it. Keep the lap wet.

Rubber Bonded Wheels

Cratex rubber bonded wheels will also smooth jade. One method that has been used with success is to smooth the stone on a coarse Cratex wheel running very wet. Then finish smoothing on wet 600 grit sanding cloth. Smoothing with fine grit rubber bonded wheels has been tried with limited success by one professional cutter.

Loose Abrasive

Most cutters advise against loose abrasive for smoothing jade because the grit usually gouges into the stone causing undercutting. A few lapidaries have used loose grit on wood laps successfully. Medium (320) and fine (400 or 600) grit are mixed with water and applied to the wood. The grit is brushed onto the lap which is run at slow speed (225 rpm for an 8-inch lap). Separate laps are used for the two grits, and everything must be washed thoroughly between grits. It is advisable to try other smoothing techniques first.

Prepolishing

The usual way to prepolish jade is to put a glaze on it in the final smoothing step. Another method of prepolishing is to use 1000 grit on a hard leather dsic. Metal lapping compound, obtainable at auto supply houses, has been used successfully. The compound consists of grit suspended in grease. If this method is used, check frequently for undercutting. If the stone undercuts, smooth it once more on fine abrasive, and omit prepolishing.

Polishing

Jade can be polished without polishing compound and buffs. Instead 4/0 flint sandpaper is used. The paper is attached to a sanding disc on which there is a sponge rubber cushion. Before polishing the paper should be broken in by sanding a hard stone until the abrasive becomes powdery. Run the disc at about 250 rpm.

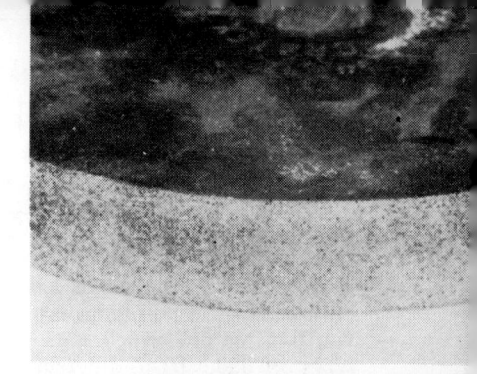

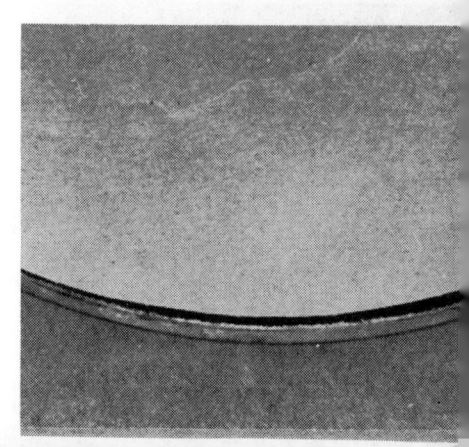

61 — ADVANCED CABOCHON CUTTING

Polishing With Buffs

Most cutters polish jade on a buff with a polishing compound. There has been much ado about which is the best buff and compound. Actually, several combinations will work. The most important step is smoothing; all the pits and crevices must be removed from the gem's surface.

Another favorite argument among experts is whether the jade should get hot or stay cool during polishing. Some contend that it must get hot so that the surface molecules will flow; others contend it should be kept cool or just warm. Both techniques produce beautifully polished gems. Several favorite polishing techniques are outlined below. Experiment until you find the one which suits your individual needs. If you polish several types of jade from different localities, you may need more than one polishing combination. *Note: In all the techniques listed, polishing powder and water are mixed to the consistency of cream. Bar forms are applied to a spinning buff, and water added occasionally.*

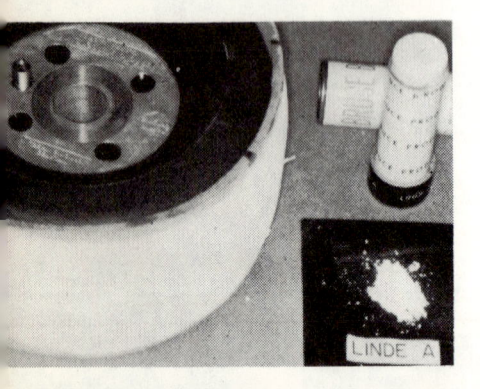

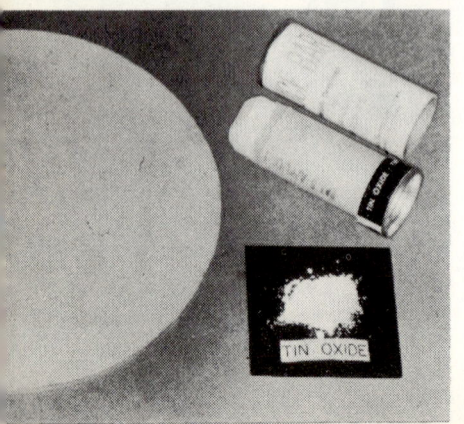

Leather Buffs

Leather is a favorite jade-polishing buff. Many cutters prefer to attach it directly to the polishing disc or drum without a cushion. Some use a sponge or felt cushion. Both the smooth and the rough side of the leather are used; it's a matter of personal preference. Some special jade buffs are available such as Rock's Jade Wheel, a metal drum covered with hard leather over a cushion. R. H. Dollar Company has a leather belt for its inflatable drum. Most manufacturers have leather circles, both hard and soft for their polishing discs.

Chrome oxide is often used on leather buffs. The powder may be mixed with water and half vinegar, and brushed on a motionless buff. Then the buff is spun until it is almost dry. The jade is applied to the buff with a fair amount of pressure to develop heat. Often the dopping wax will soften and must be cooled. Some cutters mix 1 part Linde A with 9 parts chrome oxide.

Many lapidaries now use Linde A on leather. It is much cleaner than chrome oxide. They usually let the buff run until it is almost dry, then polish. Linde A is a favorite compound for gems that undercut.

Tin oxide is sometimes used on smooth leather. The jade is not allowed to get hot.

ADVANCED CABOCHON CUTTING

Muslin Buffs

A professional cutter who polishes a lot of jade, uses a muslin buff and tin oxide. He runs the buff at 2500 rpm and keeps it fairly wet. The jade usually gets warm, but not hot. If he encounters a stone that is hard to polish, he dampens it by touching it to the buff, dips it in some Linde A powder, and applies it once more to the buff. Chrome oxide mixed with a little graphite may also be used with a muslin buff. The buff should be well covered to prevent the chrome oxide from splattering the operator and shop walls; it stains badly.

Velvet

A heavy cotton velvet that is not stainproofed should be used. Some upholstery velvet is ideal. The cloth is attached to the type of disc sander on which buffs are tied or held with springs. It should have a cushion. The tin oxide mix is brushed into the buff until the nap is saturated. Then the buff is spun until it is slightly damp. It should run between 400 and 450 rpm. Press the stone into the buff at one spot; do not move it across the surface. Add polishing compound when needed. The jade will not get hot.

Hard Felt

Hard felt is not often used because it sometimes causes jade to undercut. Occasionally jade is polished on felt with tripoli. Plenty of pressure is exerted to generate heat. Tripoli is a mild abrasive which is harder than jade; possibly its abrasive polishing action reduces undercutting. Infrequently tin oxide is used on felt to polish jade.

Wood Laps

When other polishing techniques have failed, a few cutters try wood laps. Tin oxide on soft wood is sometimes used. Heavy pressure is exerted. The lap polishes best when it is almost dry.

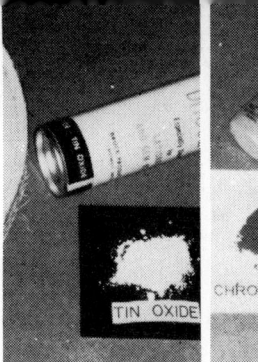

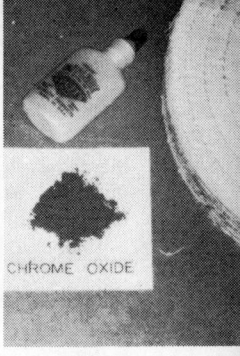

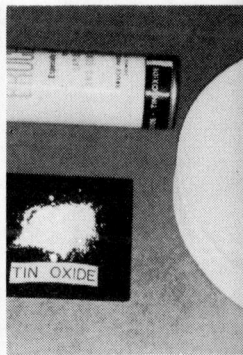

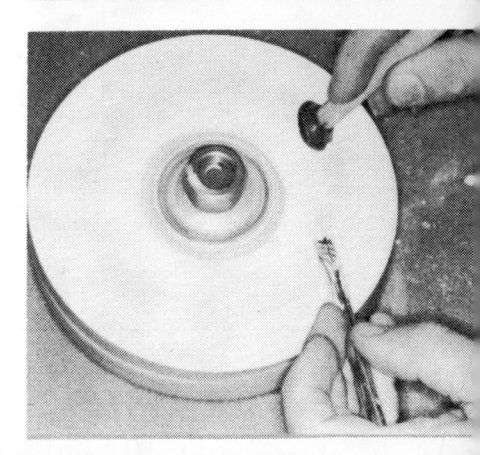

Helpful Hints

It cannot be emphasized too much that jade must be smoothed properly to take a good polish. When you have finished smoothing a piece of jade inspect it with a 10-power magnifying glass to make sure all pits and blemishes have been removed. Be sure that glazed spots do not conceal undercut areas. If you find undercut areas after polishing, repeat the last smoothing stage.

Poor quality jade will seldom polish regardless of what techniques are used. Jade with inclusions of other minerals is frequently encountered. Calcite inclusions are softer than jade, and tend to undercut. Quartz inclusions are harder, and the jade undercuts.

Jade wheels are available from dealers and Rock's Lapidary Equipment, P.O. Box 10075, San Antonio, Texas. Endless leather belts and inflatable drums are sold by dealers and distributors for R. H. Dollar Co., 316 Marion Bldg., Cleveland, Ohio.

Chrome oxide is becoming less popular as a jade polish because it is so messy. Linde A, in most cases, works well. Compared to other compounds it is expensive, but a small amount goes a long way.

Remember that jade from different areas often varies in cutting and polishing characteristics. Alaskan jade may require a different technique than that from Wyoming. Through experimentation you should find the best techniques to suit your personal touch and the varieties you encounter. It is advisable to keep a record of your findings. When you find the best technique for a particular jade, list it in the chart below:

Type Jade	Best Smoothing Technique	Best Polishing Technique

ADVANCED CABOCHON CUTTING — 64